STEAM RAIL MOTORS
OF THE
GREAT WESTERN
RAILWAY

THE
STEAM RAIL MOTORS
OF THE
GREAT WESTERN
RAILWAY

KEN GIBBS

Cover illustrations: *Front:* The first GWR steam rail motor, No. 1, and the last, No. 93 – not a replica, but a survivor, repaired and rebuilt; *Rear:* Steam rail motor no. 45.

First published 2015
Reprinted 2021

The History Press
97 St George's Place,
Cheltenham, Gloucestershire, GL50 3QB
www.thehistorypress.co.uk

British Library Cataloguing in Publication Data.
A catalogue record for this book is available from the British Library.

ISBN 978 0 7509 6103 5

Typesetting and origination by The History Press
Printed by TJ Books Limited, Padstow, Cornwall

CONTENTS

	Author's Note	6
	Acknowledgements	7
	Introduction: The Steam Rail Motor and Great Western	8
1.	The Steam Rail Motor and its Contemporaries: Britain, Empire and Beyond	15
2.	The Great Western's Rail Motors	37
3.	Steam Rail Motor Design	77
4.	Shedding Facilities for Steam Rail Motors	94
5.	The Influence of the Steam Rail Motor and the Introduction of 'Halts'	113
6.	The Branches of the GWR and the Rail motor	120
7.	The Difficulties of the Branch Lines	132
8.	The Wilkinson Report of 1925	160
9.	The Steam Rail Motor Project: A 'Last' or 'First' Chapter	168
	Epilogue	187
	References and Further Reading	188
	About the Author	190

AUTHOR'S NOTE

The last steam rail motor was taken out of service when I was about five years old, so although coming from a railway family in a railway town, I didn't see one actually in use.

From school, a completed apprenticeship at Swindon Works was followed, with thousands of others, into the RAF. On 'demob' a couple of years back on the shop floor was followed by promotion to the supervisory staff and secondment into a firm of productivity consultants just introduced to the Works (1955). It was then that I first had contact with a steam rail motor, or at least with a rail motor converted to a trailer car, and then again converted to a mobile office, positioned on a rail line directly outside the C&W Department office block at Swindon Works. The coach was subsequently moved around the Western region with me and a team for about three years, when I was once more returned to Swindon Works and the coach went on its way. Then I lost touch.

Through a working life, I had just retired (1983) and joined the Great Western Society where at Didcot I was reintroduced to my old mobile office (then as a stores for various railway items) scheduled for rebuilding into a working steam rail motor, the only survivor of its fellows. It is now fully operational and heading for a second life. I have long been involved with the dedicated groups working for the rail motor and other locomotives at Didcot, and thus the coach saga and my career seem to have turned full circle even in retirement!

ACKNOWLEDGEMENTS

Assistance in compiling this work has come from a number of sources.

The great contribution by Dr Ralph Tutton formed the basis for the rebuild of 'No. 93'. Also thanks to Tim Brian (then Curator of 'STEAM', the Museum of the Great Western Railway) who first pointed me in the direction of Dr Tutton's archive material. John Walter, who had additional engineering drawings listed on his computer and who again pointed me to the sources and obtained some of the prints for me.

To the Great Western Society at Didcot and to 'STEAM', The Museum of the Great Western Railway, for access to their archives.

Photographs are by the author unless noted otherwise.

I also have a personal connection with No. 93 both before and during the rebuild project.

My sincere thanks to all.

Ken Gibbs LCGI (Mech Eng)

No. 93 – sole survivor. (Photo D. Feltham)

INTRODUCTION

A transport innovation at the beginning of the twentieth century created great interest in many of the world's railways. The carriage with a steam engine in one end captured imaginations, none more so than the Great Western's. The birth of the steam rail motor was seen to herald a revolution in rural transport.

Its introduction on the Great Western was an astonishing success, opening up villages and market towns with potential additional travelling facilities. The problem was it was *too* successful, opening up a market with which the steam rail motors could not cope, a situation which soon became very obvious when required loads proved too much for the small power units, although they could handle a trailer car.

If something went wrong with the steam power unit, or with the carriage section, the whole rail motor was 'off the schedule' and a new thinking was required for the whole system. So started the conversions! After being in operation for five or six years only, selected rail motors had the steam unit removed, the carriages converted to trailer cars now powered by a small, separate locomotive that could also be used independently, for example shunting wagons, which the rail motor could not really take.

In the period 1914–18, war retarded the conversion programme to a degree, but following the war, by the early 1930s, the steam rail motor on the Great Western was history.

This book covers the Great Western's involvement in the rise and fall of the steam rail motor and a century later, a steam rail motor rebuild. But read on!

Businesses the world over have been and are still always on the lookout for ways of cutting costs. In this respect the railway systems of Britain and the world were no exceptions. In the first flush of railway building, many routes were established that, as time went by, although essential and to a reasonable extent still profitable, were still thought to be capable of further economies, and exertions were made to determine suitable means. All this was against a rising tide of opposition in the burgeoning field of road motor transport. As various railways continued to experiment with the old idea of the self-contained powered coach, and after trying out a borrowed example, the

Chairman of the Great Western, Earl Cawdor, announced to the 13 August 1903 meeting of shareholders:

> We are putting on a motor car service, a combined car which will carry fifty-two passengers. This car will run on the rails of our own line. We are putting on one now and it will be working in October between Stonehouse and Chalford in the Stroud Valley. We can run this car on the line, stopping not only at stations, but with the sanction of the Board of Trade, at level crossings and at roads coming up to the line … This motor car will be working by steam, there are others which are worked by petrol, but we have decided on one propelled by steam, and we hope it will be running by next October.

As good as his word, two cars started the run on 12 October 1903. There were four stops besides the Brimscombe and Stroud stations, but difficulties were soon experienced with passenger access and egress at the four intermediate stops. Down to ground level was quite a drop and the collapsible iron steps provided for this purpose (controlled from inside the car by a lever) were soon found to be rather inconvenient, particularly for long-skirted lady travellers. So, in this respect it was back to the drawing board, and the raised 'Halt' platform was proposed, an innovation detailed later in this book. However, the inaugural run was very successful and the invited distinguished guests and a host of reporters were well satisfied. Those attending the run included Mr G. Churchward (Loco & Carriage Superintendent), Mr W. Dawson (Outdoor Assistant Superintendent), Mr C. Aldington (representing the General Manager – Mr J.C. Inglis), Mr Marillier (Carriage Department), Mr Simpson (of the Superintendent of the Lines' Office) and Mr W. Waister (Locomotive & Carriage Running Department). The accompanying journalists were mainly from London and Gloucester and all were entertained to lunch on their return to Swindon. A short speech from Mr Dawson thanked those who attended the launch of the project and a reply from *The Times'* representative wished the project every success.

A further snippet of information from *The Stroud Journal & Cirencester Gazette* of Friday 9 October 1903 mentioned receipt of the official rail motor timetable. Starting from Chalford at 8 a.m. and from Stonehouse at 8.30 a.m. the motors ran an hourly service up to 10.30 p.m. from Chalford and Stonehouse 11.00 p.m., these two latter being 'late' trains on Fridays and Saturdays. The return fare between Stroud and Stonehouse was 4 pence and between Stroud and Chalford 6 pence and the duration of actual travelling twenty-three minutes between six stops (St Mary's Crossing, Brimscombe, Ham Mill Crossing, Stroud, Downfield Crossing and Ebley Crossing).

The early years of the steam rail motor saw a proliferation of use throughout the country but not so enthusiastically on the other railways of Britain (and indeed other countries), this being a time of general enthusiasm for the self-contained, steam-powered railway carriage throughout the rail scene, although other forms of power were being introduced at this time.

The extract below from the months of May and June 1908 from the train service minutes gives an idea of how the steam rail motors of the Great Western Railway (GWR) were being integrated into the system. It is possible that the idea of the rail motors substituting more cheaply for the usual trains was not progressing as had been hoped, the rail motors as shown by the example allowing only a minuscule reduction in train mileage – although the added convenience for passengers cannot be quantified in financial terms! The problems of breakdowns and maintenance would also raise its head.

However, at this early stage the enthusiasm was still there as the rail motors spread throughout the GWR system. The use of rail motors on the branches posed several problems not really related to the suburban and main-line application and are dealt with separately in later pages.

From their introduction to the GWR in 1903, the rail motor allocation to the various sheds of the system shows clearly, over almost the thirty or so years of their existence, how they rose to prominence and then faded away as their importance declined. From a 1925 report, detailed later in this work, it was shown that their popularity on other railway systems had also declined rather rapidly over the years and that currently, of ninety-one in use throughout the rail network of the country, fifty-three were still in use on the GWR, a total that would reduce and vanish in the next ten years, although at that time they were grimly clinging on to existence.

From the end of 1934 the last of the series of GWR-designed steam rail motors were shunted into the sidings of the Swindon Works for assessment. The reduction in numbers over the years from about 1917 resulted in three sold, eighteen scrapped and seventy-eight converted to trailers for the 'auto train', the successor to the steam rail motor. This conversion would entail removal and disposal of the engine unit, and a rebuild of the driving end of the rail motor to match its opposite end, the 0-4-0 engine replaced by a standard-carriage four-wheel bogie. Thus while no longer considered a viable proposition as a separate unit, the steam rail motor coach body would still be in service either as an ordinary coach, or as a trailer coach coupled to a small tank engine with the engine controllable either from the footplate or, without running round the coach and being coupled the opposite end, from the vestibule at the opposite end of the attached coach, to which a prominent warning bell was fitted.

It seems ironic that at the opposite end of the century the idea of small, fast, convenient rural and suburban rail transport had been resurrected with the introduction of the three-car diesel multiple unit – its steam motor forebears on the GWR having been abandoned in the 1930s as non-economic faced with road motor opposition, while, for example, some companies continued to develop the steam rail motor with three-car steam units as the later diesel version and were still selling them worldwide.

APPENDIX

TO

MAY AND JUNE TRAIN SERVICE MINUTES.

RAIL MOTOR-CAR SERVICES.

OXFORD SUBURBAN SERVICE.

A New Rail Motor Service has been established in the Oxford District, and new Halts were opened at Wolvercot, Hinksey, Abingdon Road, Iffley, Garsington Bridge and Horsepath.

MILEAGE STATEMENT.

PARTICULARS.	MILES.
7.20 a.m. Oxford to Wheatley	7¾
8. 5 a.m. Wheatley to Oxford	7¾
8.47 a.m. Oxford to Shipton	18¼
9.48 a.m. Shipton to Oxford	18¼
1. 3 p.m. Oxford to Princes Risboro'	21
2.10 p.m. Princes Risboro' to Oxford	21
3.57 p.m. Oxford to Kidlington	5½
4.15 p.m. Kidlington to Oxford	5½
4.40 p.m. Oxford to Princes Risboro'	21
6.33 p.m. Princes Risboro' to Oxford	21
8.15 p.m. Oxford to Thame	15¼
9. 5 p.m. Thame to Oxford	15¼
8. 8 a.m. Oxford to Bletchington	7¾
8.33 a.m. Bletchington to Oxford	7¾
9.20 a.m. Oxford to Bletchington	7¾
9.59 a.m. Bletchington to Oxford	7¾
10.25 a.m. Oxford to Wheatley	7¾
11. 0 a.m. Wheatley to Oxford	7¾
12. 2 p.m. Oxford to Heyford	11¾
12.53 p.m. Heyford to Oxford	11¾
1.55 p.m. Oxford to Blenheim	9¼
2.52 p.m. Blenheim to Oxford	9¼
5.33 p.m. Oxford to Kidlington	5½
5.50 p.m. Kidlington to Oxford	5½
11. 5 p.m. Oxford to Blenheim / 11.33 p.m. Blenheim to Oxford } Saturdays only 18½ ÷ 6 =	3
Total increase ...	280

Three additional Cars required.

Commenced February 1st. 1908

COMPARATIVE TABLE OF RAIL MOTOR-CARS PUT ON, AND TRAIN MILES SAVED. (MAY & JUNE 1908)

Date Commenced.	PARTICULARS.	May and June.	
		Cars put on.	Trains Saved.
		Increase.	Decrease.
	RAIL MOTOR-CARS IN PLACE OF TRAINS.		
	RAIL MOTOR-CARS AUGMENTING TRAIN SERVICE.		
~~Oct. 1st~~	~~Ealing and Wycombe Line and Hayes Service~~	~~19½~~	—
Feb. 1st	Oxford Suburban Service	280	—
Oct. 1st	Tavistock Branch Service	66	—
July 1st	Plymouth Suburban Service	5	—
Nov. 1st	Plymouth Suburban Service	5	—
Oct. 1st	Yealmpton Branch Service (Sundays)	3½	—
Oct. 1st	Penzance and Redruth Local Service		
Oct. 1st	Fishguard, Milford Haven and Tenby Se		
Oct. 18th	8.30 a.m. Fishguard Harbour to Neyland		
	60 ÷ 6 =		
July 1st	Llangollen and Corwen		
July 1st	Oswestry Branch		
July 1st	Chester and Ruabon		
	RAIL MOTOR-CARS OVER		

COMPARATIVE TABLE OF RAIL MOTOR-CARS PUT ON, AND TRAIN MILES SAVED—*continued.*

Date Commenced.	PARTICULARS.	May and June.	
		Cars put on.	Trains Saved.
		Increase.	Decrease.
	RAIL MOTOR-CAR SERVICES OVER MINERAL LINES.		
Jan. 1st	Gwaun-cae-Gurwen Line	21	—
July 1st	Wrexham and Coed Poeth	12½	—
Aug. 3rd	Forest of Dean Line	89½	—
Nov. 4th	Forest of Dean Line (Extension to Drybrook Halt)	20½	—
April 1st	Forest of Dean Line (Extension to and from Cinderford Joint Station)	17½	—
	TOTAL	160½	—
See Page	**RAIL MOTOR-CAR SERVICES PROPOSED FOR MAY.**		
~~30~~	~~Westbourne Park and Park Royal Early Morning Service~~	18½	—
~~30~~	~~Victoria, Clapham Junction and Greenford, and Paddington~~		
	~~and Greenford Service—Sundays 708 ÷ 9 ÷ 6 =~~		
31	Swansea to Vale of Neath Evening Service	13	—
31	Minor proposals	3	—
		14¼	—
	Less		
32	Rail Motor-Cars to be discontinued for May	48½	—
		43	
	TOTAL INCREASE	5¼	—

PARTICULARS.	May and June.	
	Cars put on.	Trains saved.
	Increase.	Decrease.
MILEAGE SUMMARY.		
RAIL MOTOR-CARS AUGMENTING TRAIN SERVICE	598½	10
RAIL MOTOR-CAR SERVICES OVER MINERAL LINES	160½	—
RAIL MOTOR-CAR SERVICES PROPOSED FOR MAY	5¼	—
	773½	10
TOTAL INCREASE RAIL MOTORS	773½	—
TOTAL DECREASE TRAINS	—	10

SWANSEA TO VALE OF NEATH EVENING SERVICE.

At present the last Train from Swansea to the Vale of Neath Line stations leaves at 8.35 p.m., and it is felt that a later service which would allow visitors to the seaside to patronise the sea trips would be appreciated.

It is therefore proposed to give a later service on Saturdays, by running a Rail Motor-Car from Neath to Glyn Neath at 10.50 p.m., in connection with the 10.15 p.m. Train from Swansea, due at Neath at 10.38 p.m.

MILEAGE STATEMENT. (MAY & JUNE 1908)

PARTICULARS.	MILES.
10.50 p.m. Neath to Glyn Neath and back, Saturdays only, 18 ÷ 6 = ...	3
Total increase	3

FOREST OF DEAN LINE.

The service over this section was extended to Drybrook Halt, commencing November 4th last, necessitating an increase of 29½ miles daily.

Commencing on April 1st, a new loop will be opened between Bilson Junction and Cinderford Joint Station, and the Cars will run to and from the Joint Station instead of calling at Bilson Halt. The increase in the mileage will be 17½ miles daily over the above.

EXTRA RAIL MOTOR-CARS PROPOSED TO BE PUT ON BEYOND THE SCHEMES BEFORE MENTIONED.

Car.	From	To	Particulars of Alterations.	Mileage.	Reasons for Alterations.
			WEEK DAYS.		
5.40 p.m. Empty	Laira Junction	Plympton			
6. 5 p.m.	Plympton	Royal Albert Bridge	} Saturdays, 12¾ ÷ 6 = 2		(To give additional service for heavy
6.20 p.m.	Royal Albert Bridge	Millbay ...		1¼	(traffic on Saturday evenings.
Less 7.30 p.m. Empty	Laira Junction	Millbay ...	Saturdays, 2¾ ÷ 6 =	¼	
5.50 p.m.	Plymouth	Keyham ...	} Saturdays only, 5 ÷ 6 =	1	To relieve 4.19 p.m. from Truro.
6.14 p.m.	Keyham ...	Plymouth			(Service re-arranged and Train mileage
8.36 a.m.	Johnston ...	H'fordwest	}	9¼	{ saved. See page 8.
8.50 a.m.	H'fordwest	Johnston ...			(To provide an earlier service from
6.50 a.m.	Kidder- minster	Bewdley ...			Bewdley to Birmingham for Week-end
7. 5 a.m.	Bewdley ...	Kidder- minster	} Mondays only, 7 ÷ 6 =	1¼	Visitors who now have to return on Sunday evenings.
			SUNDAYS.		
5.23 p.m.	Bewdley ...	Highley ...	} 12 ÷ 6 = ... 2		(To give a service from South Stafford-
5.45 p.m. Less	Highley ...	Bewdley ...		1	{ shire district to Highley on Sunday
5.22 p.m.	Bewdley ...	Stourport	} 5¼ ÷ 6 = ... 1		(evenings.
5.35 p.m.	Stourport	Bewdley ...			
			Total increase ...	14¼	

1

THE STEAM RAIL MOTOR AND ITS CONTEMPORARIES: BRITAIN, EMPIRE AND BEYOND

The enthusiasm for the steam rail motor on the GWR was never matched by similar enthusiasm on the many other rail systems throughout the country, although a number had experimented with various designs of cars. This is evidenced by a look at the Board of Trade return a decade after the 1903 introduction on the GWR. As the following list shows, no-one came anywhere near the number of rail motors running on the GWR.

		Carrying Capacity	
	In England & Wales	No.	Seats
1	Alexandra Docks & Railway	1	54
2	Barry	2	104
3	Cardiff	2	128
4	Freshwater, Yarmouth & Newport	1	12
5	Furness	1	48
6	Great Central	4	206
7	Great Northern	6	296
8	Great Western	100	5,635
9	Kent & East Sussex	1	36
10	Lancashire & Yorkshire	17	936
11	London & North Western	7	336
12	London & South Western	25	1,130
13	London, Brighton & South Coast	3	144
14	North Eastern	5	126
15	North Staffordshire	3	141
16	Rhymney	1	64
17	South Eastern & Chatham	8	448
18	Taff Vale	16	847
	TOTALS	**203**	**10,691**

SCOTLAND				
1	Caledonian		1	25
2	Glasgow & South Western		3	120
		TOTALS	**4**	**145**
IRELAND				
1	Belfast & County Down		3	184
2	Midland Great Western of Ireland		1	12
3	Midland (Irish Sections)		2	46
		TOTALS	**6**	**242**
		OVERALL TOTALS	**213**	**11,078**

There were at this time a surprising number of electric versions in existence, although some would come under the classification of tramcars. Those are included in the following list:

		Carrying Capacity	
	In England & Wales	**No.**	**Seats**
1	Blackpool & Fleetwood Tramroad	37	2,032
2	Central London	64	2,576 + coaches
3	Great Central (electric tramcars)	12	672
4	Great Western	20	960 + coaches
5	Lancashire & Yorkshire	74	5,027 + coaches
6	Liverpool Overhead	58	3,543 + coaches
7	London & South Western	17	802 + coaches
8	London, Brighton & South Coast	50	3,436 + coaches
9	London Electric	168	7,056 +coaches
10	Mersey	24	1,152 + coaches
11	Metropolitan	142	6,514 +coaches
12	Metropolitan District	206	9,768
13	Midland	68	3,492
14	North Eastern	66	3,402
	TOTALS	**1,006**	**58,477**
SCOTLAND			
1	Great North of Scotland	No	details
	TOTALS	**-**	

IRELAND			
1	Great Northern of Ireland	11	682 +1 goods car
2	Bearbrook & Newry Tramway (light railway)	2	60
3	Great Southern & Western	No	details
4	Dublin, Wicklow & Wexford later Dub'n & Sth East'n	No	details
	TOTALS	13	740
	OVERALL TOTALS	1,019	51,219

Others

1	Isle of Wight Central		
2	Port Talbot		
3	Isle of Man		

Certain of the companies listed, such as the Welsh and Bristol & Exeter, were absorbed by the GWR prior to the amalgamation, thus bringing steam railcars with them. As an example of various other steam rail motor designs, all around the period of introduction of the GWR's own, the Taff Vale Railway was among the first to sing its praises, the designs shown in the following illustrations. Mr T. Hurry Riches, the company's Locomotive and Carriage Engineer had designed and supervised construction of the vehicle at the company's Works at Cardiff. This car was produced before the GW's No. 1 appeared. Such was its success that six more were the basis of a tender to various companies, the successful bidders being the Bristol Wagon & Carriage Works Company working with the Avonside Engine Company. To discuss the successful introduction of the design, a meeting was held with Taff Vale, GWR and London & South Western Railway (LSWR) representatives at which notes were compared on operating such vehicles. By the time of the amalgamation of 1923, with the Taff Vale already absorbed by the GW, Taff Vale official returns of rail motors for 1919 show 'eighteen', for 1920 'eighteen out of use', and all have disappeared completely from the returns of 1921. A number of other Welsh railways had introduced rail motors, and the Port Talbot Railway & Docks Company had been the only absorbed company (1908) that had included an operational rail motor. This had been built by Hawthorn Leslie & Company in 1906, the coach body by Hurst, Nelson & Company. Withdrawn in July 1920 and sold to the Port of London Authority, it was withdrawn in 1926 and broken up in 1928.

The Rhymney Railway had two rail motors designed by Mr C.T. Hurry Riches (father of the Taff Vale's Mr T. Hurry Riches), which had Hudswell Clarke power units with coachwork by Cravens Limited of Sheffield. One was converted to an ordinary coach during 1910 and the other disappeared from the schedule in 1919. The engine portions were converted to 0-6-0 tank locomotives, both being taken off the stock list in 1925, being the only 0-6-0 wheel format steam railcars. The Glasgow Railway and Engineering Company built two rail motors for the Alexandra Docks & Railway Company in 1904/5. One car was converted to a coach in 1922, and, like the one on the Rhymney Railway, the other disappeared from the schedules in 1917.

The Barry Railway had two North British Locomotive Company cars built in 1905, in appearance closely resembling the GWR versions, but both were withdrawn and converted to trailers.

Also of similar design to those of the GWR suburban cars, the Cardiff Railway had two rail motors built by the Gloucester Railway Carriage & Wagon Company, with Sissons & Co supplying three power units (one spare) during 1911. Two trailer cars were also supplied by the Gloucester firm. The rail motors were converted to trailers during 1917, the power units surviving for several years before they also faced the oxy-cutting torch for scrap.

Although long before the general introduction of the steam rail motor at the beginning of the twentieth century, the Bristol & Exeter Railway had pre-empted the GWR with a version to the broad gauge of Brunel in 1848, this being the second such innovation in the country (see illustration on page 30). Ordered by Mr Gregory from the Fairfield Works at Bow, it had a trial run on the West London Railway before transfer to the Tiverton branch. Starting work on the GWR on 1 May 1849, it was eventually sold out of the service during 1856, its fate from there being unknown.

Thus were the railways all over the country involved, from very early on in some cases, in the self-contained, powered railway coach, which was introduced and was very successful, possibly too successful, and made itself in effect redundant as events and requirements overtook its power.

To conclude this section, and having outlined some of the cars in use on the British rail system, the illustrations that follow show also examples of the steam railcars in use abroad, in corners of the old Empire. The cars illustrated on the following pages show the three main types which had emerged from the experiments with the powered carriage, and were representative of those in use literally throughout the railway world of the period.

Types:
(a) The separate locomotive with carriage(s) attached, the loco either pulling a single coach or being sandwiched between two coaches.
(b) The integral locomotive style with built-in power unit, which actually looked like a small locomotive with boiler exposed but was a part of the body of the vehicle.
(c) The completely built-in power unit of special design but hidden within the contours of the carriage. In this case the steam generator could be either a loco-style boiler, a special variation of such a boiler (such as the Alexandra Docks example), or a vertical boiler, variations of which were used for stationary and steam-crane applications. The GWR version is detailed on page 63.

Type (a) shows the emerging embryo of the auto train.

Some car types Illustrated on the following pages	
Midland Railway	Class 1 – Auto steam car. Combined engine and car. Class 2 – Pullman car with separate locomotive. Class 3 – Short motor train.
North Staffordshire Railway	Ordinary type. Combined engine and car.
North Eastern Railway	Petrol electric driven rail auto-cars. Petrol engine driving electric generator. Short motor train.
Port Talbot Railway	Ordinary type. Combined engine and car.
Rhymney Railway	Ordinary type. Combined engine and car.
South Eastern & Chatham Railway	Ordinary type. Combined engine and car. Also short motor trains.
Taff Vale Railway	Ordinary type. Combined engine and car. Also short motor trains.
Dublin & South Eastern Railway (Ireland)	Short motor train type only.
Great Northern Railway (Ireland)	Short motor train type only.
Central South African Railways	Class 1 – Ordinary type. Combined engine and car. Class 2 – Small locomotive coupled by a Gould coupler to an ordinary coach.
South Australian Government Railways	Ordinary type. Combined engine and car.
Great Indian Peninsula Railway	Ordinary type. Combined engine and car.
Madras & Southern Mahratta Railway	Ordinary type. Combined engine and car.
North Western State Railway of India	Ordinary type. Combined engine and car.

Also included on pages following is a technical analysis of the contemporary cars illustrated including the general GWR version for comparison.

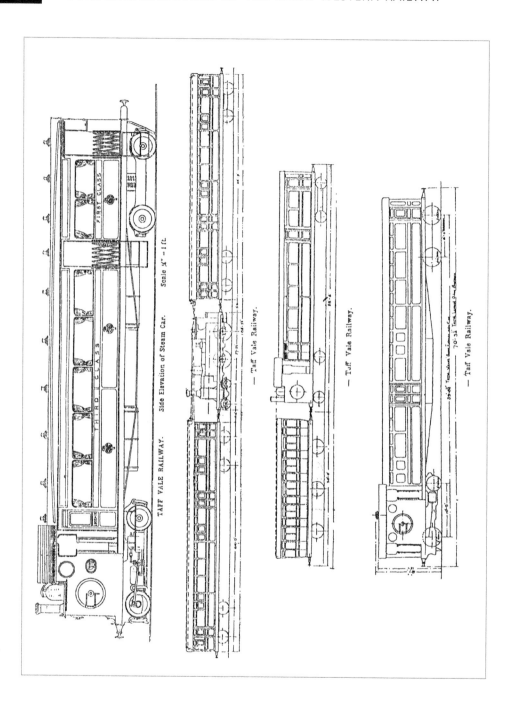

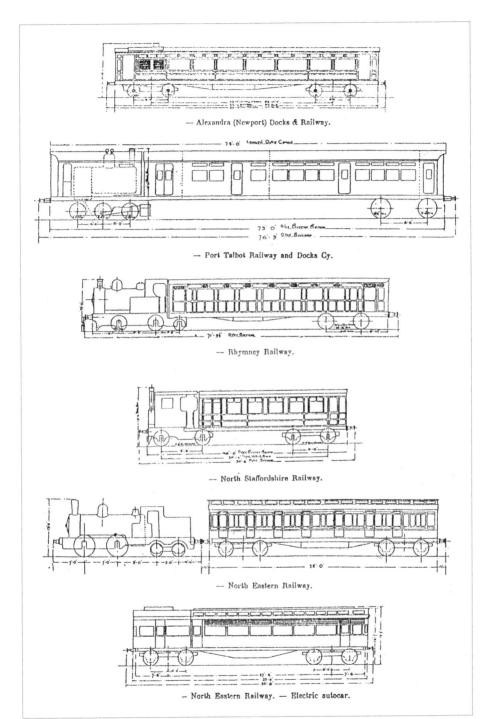

— Alexandra (Newport) Docks & Railway.

— Port Talbot Railway and Docks Cy.

— Rhymney Railway.

— North Staffordshire Railway.

— North Eastern Railway.

— North Eastern Railway. — Electric autocar.

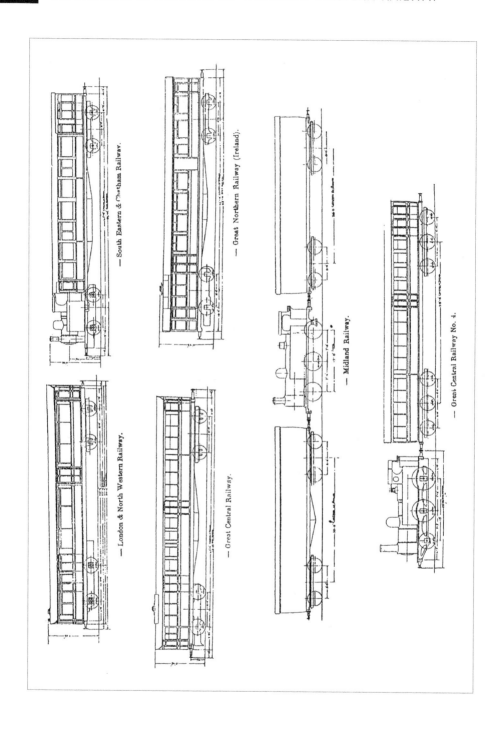

— South Eastern & Chatham Railway.

— Great Northern Railway (Ireland).

— Midland Railway.

— Great Central Railway No. 4.

— London & North Western Railway.

— Great Central Railway.

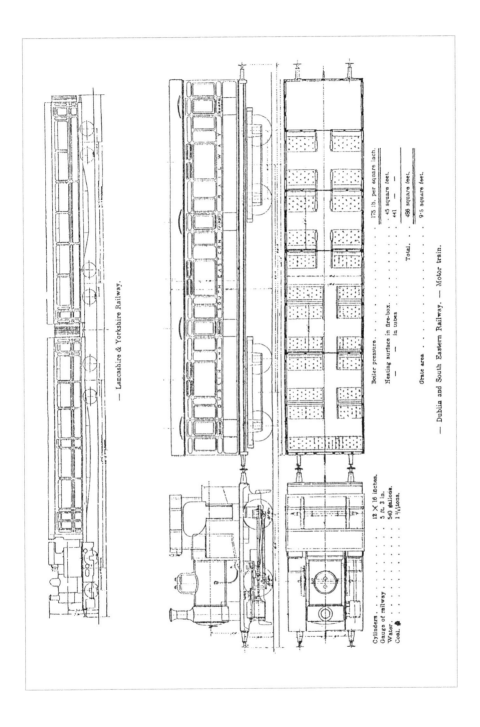

— Lancashire & Yorkshire Railway.

— Dublin and South Eastern Railway. — Motor train.

Cylinders . . . . 12 × 16 inches.
Gauge of railway . . . . . . 5 ft. 3 in.
Water . . . . 540 gallons.
Coal . . . . 1 ¼ tons.

Boiler pressure . . . . 175 lb. per square inch.
Heating surface in fire-box . . . . 45 square feet.
— — in tubes . . . . . . 441 —
                              Total . . 486 square feet.
Grate area . . . . 9·5 square feet.

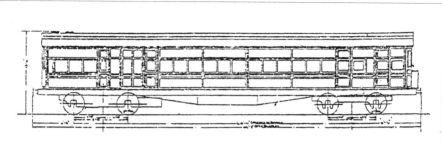

— East Indian Railway.

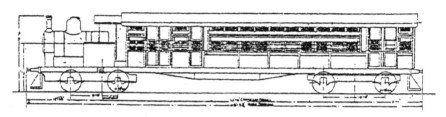

— Madras & Southern Mahratta Railway.

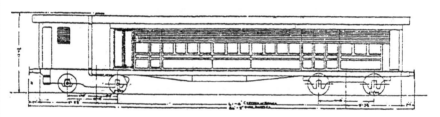

— North Western Railway (India). — Steam motor cars.

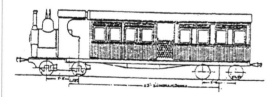

— South Australian Railway. — 3 ft. 6 in. gauge.

QUESTIONS

RAILWAYS.	2 and 3		4		5	6				
	Design.	Weight.	Length of rail.	Number of sleepers to each rail.	Weight of ordinary carriage same capacity as motor-cars.	Class and number of seats.				Luggage.
						First.	Second.	Third.	Total.	
Alexandra (Newport) Docks & Railway .	Fig. 7.	36, 39, 40, 43 tons respectively.	30 feet	12	...	(a) ... (b) ...	...	52 / 58	52 / 58	... / ...
Furness Railway	Fig. 25.	43 t. 7 c.	...	...	17 tons	...	...	...	...	...
Great Central Railway	Fig. 8.	44 t. 7 c.	30 or 45 feet	2 ft. 10½ in. pitch	26 tons	12	...	36	48	...
Great Western Railway	Figs. 11-13.	...	...	...	33 t. 10 c.	...	...	...	...	340 cubic feet.
Lancashire & Yorkshire Railway . . .	Fig. 14.	47 t. 10 c.	30 feet	11	21 t. 5 c.	...	...	56	56	...
London & North Western Railway . .	Fig. 15.	43 t. 8 c.	30 and 60 feet	12 and 24	20 t. 0 c.	...	...	48	48	598 cubic feet. / 83 square feet. / 92 square feet.
London, Brighton & South Coast Railway .	...	...	...	...	26 t. 10 c.	Class 1 : ...... / Class 2 : ...... / Class 3 :	...	60 / 40 / 48 / 48	60 / 40 / 48 / 48	... / ...
Midland Railway	Fig. 26.	...	...	...	17 t. 10 c.	Class 1 : ...... / Class 2 : 6 : .. / Class 3 : 12 : ..	...	64 / 46 / 80	64 / 52 / 92	... / ...
North Staffordshire Railway . . .	Fig. 20.	34 t. 15½ c.	...	...	16 t. 10 c.	...	...	40	40	Nil.
North Eastern Railway	Fig. 22.	47 t. 2 c.	...	...	23 t. 10 c.	...	...	52	52	Nil.
Port Talbot Railway	Fig. 23.	...	...	...	25 t. 0 c.	...	...	58	58	...
Rhymney Railway	Fig. 24.	...	30 feet	11	25 t. 0 c.	...	...	...	...	Nil.
South Eastern & Chatham Railway . .	Fig. 16.	35 t. 14 c. / 44 t. 11 c.	...	...	19 t. 14 c.	(a) 12 / (b) 16	...	56	56	7 ft. x 6 ft. 6 in.
Taff Vale Railway	Figs. 29 & 30.	40 tons	45 feet	18	15 to 20 tons	...	...	40 / 57	52 / 73	2 tons
Dublin & South Eastern Railway . .	Fig. 34.	44 t. 15 c. / 47 t. 10 c.	30 feet	10	25 tons	28	24 / 48	...	52 / 48	32·5 sq. ft. / 35·5 sq. ft.
Great Northern Railway (Ireland) .	Figs. 15 & 36.	...	Fig. 35.	...	23 tons	9	13	...	22	Nil.
Central South African Railways . .	...	...	...	...	...	8	...	54	62	..
South Australian Government Railways .	Fig. 40.	...	...	...	12 t. 10 c.	...	...	...	...	Nil.
Great Indian Peninsula Railway . .	...	20 t. 1 c.	...	...	30 t. 0 c.	14	...	70	84	Ditto.
Madras & Southern Mahratta Railway .	Fig. 37.	27 t. 0 0	30 feet	11	11 t. 10 c.	...	...	54	...	Ditto.
North Western State Railway of India .	Fig. 39.	38 t. 11 c.	...	...	24 t. 0 c.	...	...	70	...	...

RAILWAYS.	QUESTION 7. — Brake-gear		QUESTION 8. — Heating and Lighting	
	Description.	How acts.	Heating.	Lighting.
Alexandra (Newport) Docks & Railway Company.	Steam and Screw.	Steam acts on 4 wheels at boiler end. Screw acts on all wheels.	Live steam.	Acetylene gas and electricity. Outside lamps oil.
Furness Railway	Automatic Vacuum.	On all wheels.	Ditto.	Electric; outside lamps oil.
Great Central Railway	Automatic Vacuum and Screw.	On all wheels except leading wheels of independent engine.	• Gould's - steam.	Stones electric.
Great Western Railway	Ditto.	On all wheels.	Steam.	Incandescent oil gas. Petroleum, front and end lamps.
Lancashire & Yorkshire Railway	Ditto.	On all wheels. Separate screw brakes for engine and coach bogies to act as a stand by.	Gould's heaters.	Incandescent gas Footplate, front and tail lamps-oil
London & North Western Railway	Automatic Vacuum and hand.	On all wheels.	Steam.	Electric.; Front and tail lamps oil.
London, Brighton & South Coast Railway.	Westinghouse and hand.	Ditto.	Nil.	Stones' electric.
	Class 1 : Vacuum. Class 2 : Vacuum and steam. Class 3 : Ditto.	Steam brake on engine. All wheels braked except engine bogie. All wheels on Pullman car-vacuum brake.	Footwarmers.	Gas.
Midland Railway		Steam brake on engine. Vacuum brake on coaches.	Ditto.	Gas. Drivers cab and outside lamps oil.
North Staffordshire Railway	Automatic Vacuum.	Acts on all wheels.	Steam (Laycocks).	Electricity. Petroleum outside lamps.
North Eastern Railway.	Hand brake and Electro-Magnetic Track Brake.	Hand brake on one bogie only. Magnetic brake on both bogie wheels.	By radiator pipes of petrol engine.	Electricity.
Port Talbot Railway	Hand, Steam and Vacuum.	Hand brake at either end. Steam brake on engine wheels only. Vacuum on all wheels.	Gould's system.	Ditto.
Rhymney Railway.	Westinghouse and hand.	Westinghouse on all wheels excepting engine trailer wheels. Hand on engine leading and driving wheels and car bogie wheels.	Footwarmers.	Stones electric. Leading end of engine oil lamps.
South Eastern & Chatham Railway	Automatic Vacuum and Screw.	On all wheels.	Footwarmers.	Stones' Electric. Front and tail lamps oil.
Taff Vale Railway	Automatic Vacuum Steam and hand brake.	Ditto.	Steam. G. D. Peters system.	Incandescent oil gas. Oil lamp for drivers cab and outside lamps.
Dublin & South Eastern Railway	Automatic Vacuum and hand.	Ditto.	Steam.	Incandescent gas. Head tail and side lamps oil.
Great Northern Railway (Ireland).	Automatic Vacuum and hand brake.	Ditto.	Steam. Gould's system.	Stone's electric.
Central South African Railways.	Automatic Vacuum and hand brake.	On driving pair of wheels only of locomotive and all wheels of coach bogies.	Steam. Laycocks system.	Ditto.
South Australian Railways	Westinghouse and hand.	All wheels.	Nil.	Stone's electric for car. Head and tail lamps oil.
Great Indian Peninsula Railway.	Automatic and hand.	Ditto.	Nil.	Electric.
Madras & Southern Mahratta Railway.	Vacuum and hand.	Ditto.	Nil.	Gas inside car and outside car lamps. Outside lamps on engine oil.
North Western State Railway of India.	Vacuum Screw and Steam.	Vacuum on trailing end only. Screw on both bogies. Steam-engine end only.	Nil.	Gas and oil lamps.

QUESTION 10. — Boiler.

RAILWAY.	Type.	Grate area, in square feet	Tubes. Number.	Tubes. Length.	Tubes. Inner diameter.	Heating surface, in square feet. Tubes.	Heating surface, in square feet. Fire-box.
Alexandra (Newport) Docks & Railway	Locomotive type with water tubes in fire-box.	7	Smoke, 155 Water, 119	2 ft. 6 in.	1 5/16 inches.	Smoke, 152 Water, 119	76
Furness Railway	Locomotive.	12	Smoke, 226	...	1 3/4 inches external.	Smoke, 438.4	71
Great Central Railway							
Great Western Railway	Vertical cone top.			...	...		
Lancashire & Yorkshire Railway							
London & North Western Railway	Locomotive.	0·4	100	5 ft. 0 in.	1.54 inches.	455	54
Drawings.							
London Brighton & South Coast Railway — Class 1.	Ordinary locomotive.	.10	121	8 ft. 2 1/4 in.	1 9/16 inches.	463	55
— Class 2.	Special locomotive, Belpaire-box.	7	242	3 ft. 11 in.	1 3/16 inches.	327·4	41·6
Midland Railway — Class 1.	Locomotive type.	8·9	182	3 ft. 11 11/15 in.	1 1/2 inches 11-13 WG external.	291	58
— Class 2.	Ditto.	11·3	190	9 ft. 2 5/8 in.	1 1/8 inches 11-14 WG external.	754·52	67·23
— Class 3.	Ditto.	14·8	213	10 ft. 4 5/8 in.	1 3/4 inches 11-14 WG external.	1,024	91
North Staffordshire Railway	Locomotive type.	7	242	3 ft. 11 in.	1 3/4 inches 14 WG external.	328	40
North Eastern Railway	No rail _auto_ steam cars. — (See separate statement supplied.)						
Port Talbot Railway	Locomotive type 170 lb. pressure.	*13·1	...	...	...	591	69
Rhymney Railway	Locomotive type.						
South Eastern & Chatham Railway	Ditto.	8·8	167	4 ft. 9 in.	1 5/8 inches.	337	445
Taff Vale Railway — Class 1.	Locomotive type double ended.	8	299	2 ft. 3 11/16 in.	1 17/32 inches.	292·28	21·28
— Class 2.	Ditto.	10·2	464	2 ft. 3 9/16 in.	1 13/32 inches.	414·21	22·71
Dublin & South Eastern Railway							
Great Northern Railway (Ireland).	Locomotive type.	7·2	95	8 ft. 11 in.	1 5/8 inches.	425 Total including fire-box.	50·5
Central South African Railways — Class 1.	Ditto.	10·75	180	6 ft. 0 in.	1 3/8 inches.	459·5	30
— Class 2.	Ditto.	4·9	...	6 ft. 0 in.	...	117·4	
South Australian Government Railways.							
Great Indian Peninsula Railway.							
Madras & Southern Mahratta Railway	Locomotive type.	9·76	174	6 ft. 0 in.	1 5/8 inches 11 WG external.	444·15	46·19
North Western State Railway of India	Ditto.	9	164	3 ft. 6 in.	1 3/4 inches external.	252	48

RAILWAYS.		QUESTION 10. (Continue	
		Number and type of feeding apparatus.	Safety spring.
Alexandra (Newport) Docks & Railway		No. 1 car 2 injectors. No. 2 car 2 steam inspirators.	Double spring.
Furness Railway		Two No. 5 injectors.	Ramsbottom.
Great Central Railway		...	...
Great Western Railway		Two No. 6 injectors.	2 "Pop".
Lancashire & Yorkshire Railway		2 Gresham and Craven type No. 8 injectors.	One twin Ramsbott 3 inches diameter
London & North Western Railway		2 Gresham No. 5 combination injectors.	One duplex sprin safety valve.
London Brighton & South Coast Railway	Class 1.	2 C' head pumps.	2 spring balance 2 ½ inches diamete
	Class 2.	2 No. 7 Combination injectors.	Ramsbottom 2 ¼ incl
	Class 3 and 4.	...	...
Midland Railway.	Class 1.	Injectors.	Spring loaded.
	Class 2.	Ditto.	Ditto.
	Class 3.	Ditto.	Ditto.
North Staffordshire Railway		2 Gresham and Craven's No. 7 combination injectors.	Ramsbottom 2 2 ¼ incl
North Eastern Railway		...	...
Port Talbot Railway		Two 6 Millimeter Gresham and Craven.	Crosby's "Pop".
Rhymney Railway		2 injectors.	...
South Eastern & Chatham Railway		Ditto.	"Pop".
Taff Vale Railway		2 Gresham and Craven's.	Ramsbottom.
Dublin & South Eastern Railway		←	
Great Northern Railway. (Ireland)		Two No. 6 Gresham and Craven.	Crosby's "Pop" 2 ½ inches.
Central South African Railways.	Class 1.	Two injectors.	Two.
	Class 2.	Ditto.	Ditto.
South Australian Government Railways.		Two Gresham & Craven.	Two Ramsbottom.
Great Indian Peninsula Railway		Two No. 5 Gresham and Craven.	Two spring safety valh 2 inches.
Madras & Southern Mahratta Railway		Ditto.	Ramsbottom.
North Western State Railway of India		...	...

Superheating apparatus not used. No liquid fuel used.

Blower.	Blast pipe.	Pressure.	Coal used.	Cylinders.	Motion.
...	Fixed blast nozzle 1 5/8 inch diameter.	160 lb. per square inch.	Lumps.	Two 9 × 14 inches simple expansion.	...
...	Fixed 3 inches.	160 lb.	Yorkshire.	Two 11 × 14 inches simple expansion.	Walschaerts valve gear.
...	...	...	Lumps.	...	...
...	Fixed 3 1/2 inches.	160 lb.	Lumps, small and mixed.	...	...
One annular jet type.	Fixed.	180 lb.	Lumps.	Two 12 × 16 inches.	Walschaerts gear.
One steam blower.	Fixed 3 inches.	175 lb.	Lumps.	...	...
Ring.	Fixed 3 3/4 inches.	150 lb.	Welsh and Shipley.	Two 12 × 20 inches simple expansion.	Link six-coupled engine ordinary connecting rod distribution.
Ring.	Fixed 2 5/8 inches.	180 lb.	Ditto.	Two 8 1/2 × 14 inches.	Walschaerts single D.W. engine ordinary connecting rod distribution.
...	...	...	Pratt's spirit.	...	...
Ring.	Fixed 2 1/4 inches.	160 lb.	Lumps.	Two 11 × 15 inches simple expansion.	Walschaerts.
Ditto.	Fixed 4 1/4 inches.	140 lb..	Ditto.	15 × 20 inches.	Stephenson Link.
Ditto.	Fixed 4 5/8 inches.	140 lb.	Ditto.	17 × 24 inches.	Ditto.
Ditto.	Fixed 2 5/8 inches.	180 lb.	Ditto.	Two 8 1/2 × 14 inches.	Walschaerts.
...	...	...	...	...	
Ring.	Jones' Patent fixed.	170 lb.	Welsh.	Two 12 × 16 inches.	Walschaerts.
...	Fixed.	175 lb.	Ditto.	...	
Ring.	Fixed some « high » 2 1/4 inches some « low » 2 3/4 inches.	160 lb.	Bituminous Small with large proportion of dust.	Two 10 × 15 inches.	Walschaerts.
Steam blower pipe.	Fixed.	Large car 180 lb.; Small car 160 lb.	Welsh.	10 1/4 × 14 inches Large car 9 × 14 inches Small car.	...
Ordinary.	Ordinary.	175 lb.	Welsh.	Two 12 × 16 inches.	...
One blower.	Ordinary 2 3/4 inches.	160 lb.	Lump.	Two 11 × 21 3/4 inches.	« Allan » straight link
Ditto.	Ordinary 2 3/4 inches.	160 lb.	Ditto.	Two 11 × 16 inches.	Walschaerts.
Ring.	Fixed.	180 lb.	Lumpy bituminous.	Two 6 1/2 × 10 inches.	Ditto.
Ditto.	Fixed 2 1/4 inches.	170 lb.	Indian lumps.	Two.	
One blower.	Fixed 3 1/4 inches.	160 lb.	Ditto.	...	...
...	...	...	...	...	...

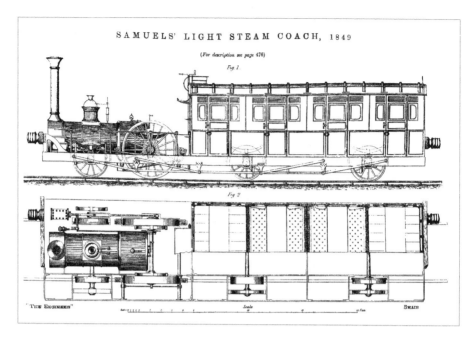

The concept of the steam rail motor that led to the flood of designs at the beginning of the twentieth century had been preceded halfway through the nineteenth with examples such as these. However, they did not catch on with designers and railway companies until much later. (Steam Picture Library)

Some other steam rail motor designs of the early twentieth century. Note the differences in layout of the power unit boiler. (Steam Picture Library)

Cardiff Railway SRM No. 1. (Steam Picture Library)

Steam rail motor of the SW, LB & SC Joint Railway. (Steam Picture Library)

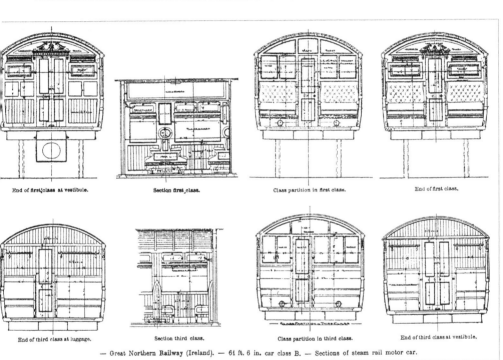

End of first class at vestibule.   Section first class.   Class partition in first class.   End of first class.

End of third class at luggage.   Section third class.   Class partition in third class.   End of third class at vestibule.

— Great Northern Railway (Ireland). — 61 ft. 6 in. car class B. — Sections of steam rail motor car.

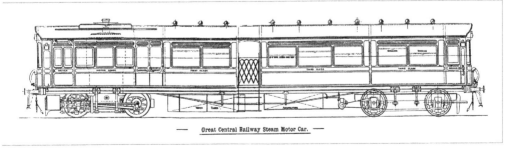

— Great Central Railway Steam Motor Car. —

Note the spoked wheels at the driving end, and 'Mansell' wheels at the training end. A design with similarity to that of the Great Western steam motors with centre entry and vertical cylindrical boiler.

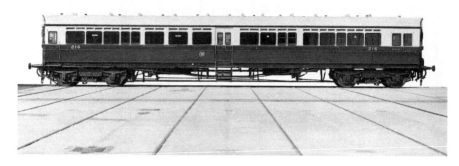

70ft trailer 216 (converted from Rail motor 64). Lot 1545, Dia A29. Neg MT37, Photo 7.10.35. (Steam Picture Library)

An example of an autotrailer's driver controls. (Steam Picture Library)

A steam rail motor and its trailer car. A complete but restricted-use unit. (Steam Picture Library)

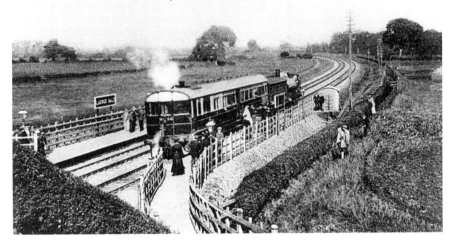

Lacock Halt and First Motor Opened Oct. 16, 1905

The steam rail motor opened up the potential of rural transport and was responsible for the establishment of the country 'halt' platforms. (Steam Picture Library)

GWR steam rail motors await their fate outside Swindon's 'A' Shop.

While in Britain the GWR steam motor story ended nominally in 1935, their popularity having waned over the previous decade and a half, at least one steam rail motor in another corner of the world was still going strong in 1999!

In Sri Lanka, on the dual-gauge Kelani Valley Line (5ft 6in and 2ft 6in), a Sentinel V2 No. 331, built in 1928, was running on the track between Colombo and Homagama (2ft 6in gauge).

The Sentinel-Cammell Rail Car 1999. (Photograph by M. Hyde)

The problem of running out of water or of water pump or injector failure, which also shows that dropping the fire brings its own hazards! (Photograph by M. Hyde)

Sentinel-Cammell steam rail car
No. 5

Sentinel-Cammell Notes

Origin: Egyptian National Railways	**Date Built:** 1951	**No:**	5208
Type: SMU	**Builder:** Metro-Cammell	**Owner:**	QRS
Status: Under Restoration	**Location:** Upyard	**Accession No:** W/0135	

Technical Details

Boiler — 335psi three-drum water-tube boiler.

Engine — Two six-cylinder single-acting compact steam engines, driving the last and first articulated bogies of the power car.

Regulator — Housed in the boiler room. Controlled by hydraulics from driving compartment at either end of the unit.

Control — 'Notching up' of engines by hydraulics from driving compartments. Series of lights to indicate regulator position and notched-up position.

Boiler Feed — Automatic with a float valve controlling a feed-water pump. Standby injector.

Fuel — Heavy Bunker C Oil which is heated, strained, reheated and blown under pressure into the boiler firebox.

Brakes — Standard Westinghouse air system.

While it continued the association with steam power, the Sentinel rail motor's power unit differed entirely from the GW power unit. This also applied to boiler feed and unit control.

It featured a three-drum water-tube boiler for 335psi steam pressure and two six-cylinder engines, more like those in a diesel rail car, and final drive by Cardan shaft. There was no comparison with the GWR version with its outside cylinders, Whalschaert valve gear, crossheads and connection rods, which was more like a conventional locomotive arrangement.

One striking feature of the Sentinel was the suspension: three cars sharing four bogies, making them inseparable. Thus it suffered the weakness inherent in all rail motors, single or joined, where any mechanical problem affected the complete unit, taking it out of the running schedule.

The use of this Sentinel, and probably the rest of those employed, appears to be of an urban, main-line commuter service essentially differing from the GWR's steam motor application on mostly rural branch lines, which showed they were not really powerful enough to operate efficiently on main commuter routes due to capacity limitations, or on branch lines due to lack of power.

One limitation of which they were all susceptible, although probably not required in the Sentinel application, was their inability to assist with the rural shunting and movement of miscellaneous loaded wagons.

For further reading see *(History of) 'The Sentinel' (Works)*, 1st Vol. 1880–1930, 2nd Vol. 1930–1980 by A.R. & J.L. Thomas. Woodpecker Publications 1987.

2

THE GREAT WESTERN'S RAIL MOTORS

Building/Purchase

The concept of a self-powered railway coach was not the brainchild of the GW's engineer, G.J. Churchward, having been in existence in various forms almost from the birth of the steam locomotive. Indeed, his first venture into the use of the rail motor began with a borrowed example, on loan from the LBSC/LSWR East Southsea service, and tried out on the route between Stroud and Cheltenham.

The LBSC Railway had gone into considerable detail and research on the possibilities of the rail motor and had commissioned a report, published in 1904, on continental comparisons of other attempts at a successful design. The report, by Mr P. Dawson MI MECH E, MIEE etc. (1904), listed and critically reviewed steam, petrol, petrol/electric and 'Accumulator'* electric cars then in use, with initial costs, running and maintenance costs and all technical comments in the designs. (*See also Tail Piece at the end of the book.)

Thus the step by the GW into the field of the rail motor was not in the dark but into a growing and broadening application. The ordering went on apace. The 12 December 1903 Board Meeting (Minute 20) agreed to the construction of twelve cars for £21,000, and again on 21 January 1904 (Minute 17) approval was given for twelve rail motor cars for branch use. The General Manager reported on 11 May 1904 (Minute 11) that all authorised rail motors were now under construction and a recommendation for another thirty should be put in hand at a cost of £50,000. These were to be twelve cars for suburban traffic, twelve cars for branch traffic and six trailer cars. These were lots 1078, 1079 (12 August 1904), 1055 (4 December 1903), 1081 (28 September 1904). By 5 October 1904 the services run by the company were analysed and a recommendation made for the construction of thirty additional rail motors and fourteen trailers. The estimated cost was £80,450 and tenders were invited from interested firms, the vehicles to be built to the approved GWR drawings. These vehicles were to be 70ft long, some to be built at Swindon. So on 20 October 1904 Board approval was given for the building of:

Lot No.	No.	Type	Place/Company
Lot 1086	6	70ft motor cars	To be built at Swindon
Lot 1089	2	70ft motor cars	To be built at Swindon
Lot 1090	2	70ft trailer cars	To be built at Swindon
Lot 1103	4	70ft trailer cars	To be built at Swindon
Lot 1087	2	59ft 6in trailer cars	To be built at Swindon
Lot 1099	2	56ft 3in motor cars*	Kerr, Stuart & Co
Lot 1100	12	70ft motor cars	Kerr, Stuart & Co
Lot 1101	8	59ft 6in motor cars	Gloucester Wagon Co
Lot 1102	6	59ft 6in trailer cars	Bristol Wagon Co

*These (shown as diagram E, plate 48) differed from the general design having small 9in diameter x 15in stroke cylinders and a boiler differing from the standard vehicle pattern. They became Nos 15 & 16 and were built at a cost of £2,073 each.

Costs of the Kerr, Stuart & Co 70ft steam rail motors were £2,500 each for the twelve. The eight 59ft 6in versions by the Gloucester Carriage & Wagon Co were £2,445 each.

Traffic Committee Minute 14 of 8 August 1906 lists approval for six more cars, three 70ft type 'M' at £2,100 each and three 70ft Type 'O' at £1,950 each.

A very interesting development recorded as Minute 11 of Wednesday 31 October 1906 meeting of the Locomotive Carriage and Wagon Committee states:

> The Locomotive Superintendent reported that in cases of extensive repairs to rail motor cars the time these vehicles are out of traffic would be considerably lessened if spare engines and boilers were available to enable those requiring a thorough overhaul to be changed, and he therefore recommended the construction of six spare motor engines and boilers at an estimated cost of £6,900.

Approval from the Board came on 1 November 1906, but the whole incident reveals the problems now being experienced with virtually new, or at most three-year-old, rail motor power units. Knowing the construction and acceptance standards of the GWR, was the engineering maybe failing due to the design? (See Chapter 3 for an overall analysis of rail motor failures and causes.) Nine more 'O' type cars at £2,100 each were ordered on 7 August 1907 but by 1908 requests for excess expenditure amounts to the Board were agreed, and included payments for the nine 'O' type cars.

By 1908, the fleet of steam rail motors was virtually complete (a modification to six cars in 1910 in the form of provision of gangways is recorded) and cars had spread throughout the GW system with, it must be said, unimaginable success. This very success was to prove rather a burden in terms of lack of power and capacity, but the railcar was off to a great start and, as an example, 2.25 million passengers were carried in the first six months of 1905 (*Railway Magazine* July/December 1905).

To keep tabulated data together the building and subsequent withdrawal dates are listed as follows:

LIFE OF THE STEAM RAIL MOTORS – Dates & Data, Building to Condemned									
SRM No.	Date Built	SRM Diagram	First Engine No.	Withdrawn	Date Converted	Trailer Diagram	Trailer No.	Trailer Condemned	
1	10/03	A	0801	6/17	6/17	A6	105	/48	
2	10/03	A¹	0802	1/17	1/17	A6	106	/52	
3	4/04	B/C	0803	6/15	6/15	Z	99	9/54	
4	4/04	B/C	0804	1/15	1/15	Z	100	4/52	
5	4/04	B/C	0805	5/15	5/15	Z	101	12/50	
6	4/04	C	0806	1/15	1/15	Z	102	11/51	
7	5/04	C	0809	1/15	1/15	Z	103	9/53	
8	5/04	C	0810	2/15	2/15	Z	104	6/52	
9	5/04	D/D¹	0811	2/16	12/16	A7	107	2/52	
10	5/04	D¹	0812	12/16	12/16	A7	108	9/54	
11	6/04	D	0814	3/17	3/17	A7	109	7/53	
12	6/04	D	0815	12/16	12/16	A7	110	9/53	
13	6/04	D	0816	3/19	3/19	A7	111	10/57	
14	7/04	D¹	0818	11/18	11/18	A7	112	5/52	
15	10/05	E	0864	4/20	SOLD WITH ENGINE 0864	-	-		
16	10/05	E	0865	12/27	NOT CONVERTED	-	-		
17	4/04	F	0807	4/19	4/19	A9	113	4/49	
18	4/04	F	0808	5/19	5/19	A9	114	9/55	
19	7/04	G	0820	8/19	8/19	A9	115	4/51	

LIFE OF THE STEAM RAIL MOTORS – Dates & Data, Building to Condemned

SRM No.	Date Built	SRM Diagram	First Engine No.	Withdrawn	Date Converted	Trailer Diagram	Trailer No.	Trailer Condemned	
20	8/04	G	0824	9/19	9/19	A9	116	11/45	
21	6/04	G	0817	5/20	5/20	A9	117	2/52	
22	7/04	G	0822	2/20	2/20	A9	118	11/57	
23	8/04	G	0823	3/20	3/20	A9	119	4/49	
24	7/04	G	0821	5/20	5/20	A9	120	4/49	
25	5/04	F	0813	4/20	4/20	A9	121	6/52	
26	6/04	G	0819	2/20	2/20	A9	122	3/55	
27	8/04	G¹	0825	3/20	3/20	A9	123	10/50	
28	9/04	G	0826	2/20	2/20	A9	124	10/52	
29	1/05	H	0835	3/20	3/20	A10	125	10/53	
30	1/05	H	0833	10/35	NOT CONVERTED		-	-	
31	12/04	J	0827	12/22	12/22		129	5/54	
32	12/04	J¹	0828	4/20	4/20	A10	128	8/57	
33	12/04	H	0830	12/22	12/22	A10	130	7/56	
34	1/05	H	0832	12/22	12/22	A10	131	6/61	
35	12/04	J	0829	12/22	12/22	A10	132	10/54	
36	12/04	H	0831	1/23	1/23	A10	133	4/51	
37	2/05	K¹	0844	10/35	NOT CONVERTED		-	-	
38	3/05	K	0848	12/27	5/28	A23	146	8/53	
39	4/05	K	0849	6/33	12/33	A23	197	1/57	
40	3/05	K	0847	6/33	3/34	A23	198	12/56	
41	1/05	L	0836	12/27	6/28	A24	147	11/57	
42	1/05	L	0834	7/20	SOLD AS STEAM RAIL MOTOR				
43	2/05	M¹	0837	4/23	4/23	A17	134	9/57	
44	2/05	M	0839	4/23	4/23	A18	135	3/58	
45	2/05		0840	12/27	5/28	A25	148	3/56	
46	2/05	M	0842	11/22	11/22	A15	136	3/39	
47	2/05	M	0843	10/22	10/22	A15	137	10/54	
48	3/05	M	0845	1/16	DESTROYED BY FIRE			1916	
49	2/05	N	0841	7/20	SOLD WITH ENGINE 0858		-	-	
50	3/05	N	0846	4/23	4/23	A19	138	5/56	

LIFE OF THE STEAM RAIL MOTORS – Dates & Data, Building to Condemned

SRM No.	Date Built	SRM Diagram	First Engine No.	Withdrawn	Date Converted	Trailer Diagram	Trailer No.	Trailer Condemned	
51	4/05	N	0850	4/23	4/23	A19	139	9/56	
52	2/05	N	0838	4/23	4/23	A19	140	12/55	
53	9/05	O	0859	6/33	12/33	A26	199	4/58	
54	9/05	O	0860	1/30	1/30	A26	181	10/58	
55	10/05	O	0865	10/35	NOT CONVERTED	-	-		
56	10/05	O	0856	1/30	1/30	A26	182	5/56	
57	9/05	O	0861	12/27	5/28	A26	149	9/56	
58	9/05	O	0857	6/33	12/33	A26	200	2/59	SOLD
59	11/05	P/T	0862	6/20	6/20	A13	126	1/55	
60	10/05	P/T	0853	6/20	6/20	A14	127	1/55	
61	3/06	O	0866	12/27	6/28	A29	150	1/56	
62	4/06	O	0867	11/29	6/30	A29	186	1/55	
63	4/06	O	0868	12/27	6/28	A29	151	5/55	
64	4/06	O	0869	1/35	12/35	A29	216	9/57	
65	4/06	O	0870	10/35	NOT CONVERTED	-	-		
66	5/06	O	0871	3/35	1/36	A29	217	9/56	
67	6/06	O	0872	12/27	6/28	A29	152	12/55	
68	6/06	O	0873	12/27	6/28	A29	153	12/54	
69	6/06	O	0874	6/33	3/34	A29	201	10/58	
70	6/06	O	0875	10/35	NOT CONVERTED	-	-		
71	6/06	O	0876	10/35	NOT CONVERTED	-	-		
72	7/06	O	0877	1/35	11/35	A29	218	11/57	
73	4/06	Q	0878	6/33	2/34	A31	202	3/56	
74	4/06	Q	0879	6/33	2/34	A31	203	3/58	Re-used to Dec '58
75	5/06	Q	0880	6/34	9/34	A31	207	12/56	
76	4/06	Q	0881	1/5	9/35	A31	219	4/56	
77	4/06	Q	0882	10/35	NOT CONVERTED	-	-		
78	6/06	Q	0883	6/34	9/34	A31	208	3/57	
79	6/06	Q	0884	6/34	9/34	A31	209	8/57	
80	6/06	Q	0885	10/35	NOT CONVERTED	-	-		
81	5/07	Q¹	0890	11/34	11/34	A31	211	3/59	
82	5/07	Q¹	0889	6/33	1/34	A31	204	4/49	Re-used to Apr '51

LIFE OF THE STEAM RAIL MOTORS – Dates & Data, Building to Condemned

SRM No.	Date Built	SRM Diagram	First Engine No.	Withdrawn	Date Converted	Trailer Diagram	Trailer No.	Trailer Condemned	
83	5/07	Q¹	0876	6/33	1/34	A31	205	8/54	
84	12/07	R	0899	3/30	3/30	A26	183	9/57	
85	12/07	R	0900	12/27	6/28	A26	154	12/56	
86	12/07	R	0897	6/33	12/33	A26	206	9/56	
87	12/07	R	0898	12/27	6/28	A26	155	9/57	
88	1/08	R	0902	10/35	NOT CONVERTED		-	-	
89	12/07	R	0903	12/27	6/28	A26	156	12/56	
90	12/07	R	0901	12/27	6/28	A26	157	8/57	
91	1/08	R	0905	1/35	8/35	A26	210	11/56	
92	1/08	R	0904	10/35	NOT CONVERTED		-	-	
93**	2/08	R	0906	11/34	5/35	A26	212	5/56	Preserved @ Didcot
94	2/08	R	0907	4/30	3/30	A26	185	9/57	
95	2/08	R	0908	3/30	3/30	A26	184	3/59	
96	2/08	R	0910	1/34	5/35	A26	213	6/56	
97	2/08	R	0912	2/35	2/35	A26	214	12/56	
98	2/08	R	0909	6/35	1/36	A26	215	12/57	
99	2/08	R	0911	12/27	5/28	A26	158	11/57	

NOTES:

(1)   Car No. 100 was a petrol/electric version. A hint of future progress?

(★★)   No. 93 survived as a mobile office and then as a stores vehicle. It was made the subject of a rebuilding programme a century later.

(2)   The diagrams refer to the car, not the interchangeable engine.

STEAM RAIL MOTOR DIAGRAMS

Lot No.	Diagram	Car No.	Type	Seating	*Dia. of Wheels	Overall Length	Total Wheelbase
1037	A	1	SUBURBAN	52	3' 7"	60' 0¾"	45' 6"
	A¹	2	SUBURBAN	52	3' 7"	60' 0¾"	45' 6"
	B	3–5	SUBURBAN	52	3' 7"	63' 6¾"	48' 9"
	C	6–8	SUBURBAN	52	3' 7"	63' 6¾"	48' 9"

Lot No.	Diagram	Car No.	Type	Seating	*Dia. of Wheels	Overall Length	Total Wheelbase
STEAM RAIL MOTOR DIAGRAMS							
	D	9–14	SUBURBAN	54	3' 7"	63' 6¾"	48' 9"
	Dᴵ	10–14	SUBURBAN	54	3' 7"	63' 6¾"	48' 9"
	⬚E	15, 16	SUBURBAN ☒	48	3' 5"	56' 3"	50' 0½"
	F	17,18,25	BRANCH	51	3' 7"	63' 6"	48' 9"
1063	G	19–24, 26, 28	BRANCH	51	3' 7"	63' 6"	45' 9"
	Gᴵ	27	BRANCH	51	3' 7½"	63' 6"	45' 9"
	H	29, 30, 33, 34, 36	BRANCH?	49	3' 7½"	63' 6"	46' 6"
	J	31–35	BRANCH? ☒ As H	49	3' 7½"	63' 6"	46' 6"
1078	Jᴵ	32	BRANCH?	49	3' 7½"	63' 6"	46' 6"
	K	38–40	BRANCH	63	3' 7½"	74' 0"	57' 3"
	Kᴵ	37	BRANCH	63	3' 7½"	74' 0"	57' 3"
1079	L	41–42	SUBURBAN	50	3' 7½"	63' 6"	46' 6"
	M	43–48	SUBURBAN	64	3' 7½"	74' 0"	57' 2"
	N	49–52	SUBURBAN	64	3' 7½"	74' 0"	57' 2"
1088	O	53-58	SUBURBAN?	61	3' 7½"	74' 0"	59' 5"
1100		(61–72*)					
1089	P	59–60	SUBURBAN?	63	3' 7½"	74' 0"	57' 3"
1101	Q	73–80	SUBURBAN?	45	3' 7½"	63' 6"	48' 11"
	Qᴵ	81–83	SUBURBAN?	45	3' 7½"	63' 6"	48' 11"
	R	84–99	SUBURBAN?	61	3' 7½"	74' 0"	59' 5"
	T	59, 60	SUBURBAN? ❹ As P	63	3' 7½"	74' 0"	57' 3"

☒ Variation only in boiler heating surface * Carrying no motor ⬚ Built by Kerr, Stuart & Co.

POWER UNIT DETAILS				
Car No.	Cylinders	Motor Wheel Dia.	Sq Ft Heating Surface	LBS Tractive Effort
1 & 2	12" x 16"	3' 8"	670	6598
3 – 14	12" x 16"	3' 6½"	672	7370
15 & 16	9" x 15"	3' 5"	350	4280
17 – 36	12" x 16"	3' 6½"	652	7370
37 – 40	12" x 16"	4' 0"	652	6350
41 & 42	12" x 16"	3' 6½"	652	7370
43 – 72	12" x 16"	4' 0"	652	6530
73 – 83	12" x 16"	4' 0"	652	6530
84 – 99	12" x 16"	4' 0"	658	6530

POWER UNIT BUILDING PROGRAMME		
Unit No.	**Year**	**Built**
0801-0802	1903	SWINDON
0803-0831	1904	SWINDON
0851-0852	1904	SWINDON
0832-0850	1905	SWINDON
0853-0858	1905	WOLVERHAMPTON
0859-0863	1905	SWINDON
0878-0887	1906	SWINDON
0888-0905	1907	SWINDON
0906-0912	1908	SWINDON

SPARE ENGINES	
Unit No.	**Built**
0851	11/04
0852	11/04
0854	7/05
0858	10/05
0863	11/05
0886	4/06
0887	8/06
0888	3/07
0891	3/07
0892	5/07
0893	9/07
0894	5/07
0895	6/07
0896	10/07

There was no guarantee that any steam railcar would finish its working life with the engine with which it started.

Tabulation from the GWR General Meeting of Proprietors up to and including 1935

Half Year	No. of Cars in Service
31/12/05	46
30/06/06	55
31/12/06	56
30/06/07	75
31/12/07	63
30/06/08	63
31/12/08	80

To 1913 gap in records.

CHANGE OF FORMAT DATA					
Year	Number	Seats	Year	Number	Seats
1913	100	5,589	1925	53	3,023
1914	100	5,589	1926	53	3,023
1915	94	5,277	1927	39	2,199
1916	90	5,051	1928	39	2,199
1917	90	5,051	1929	39	2,199
1918	86	4,839	1930	33	1,841
1919	81	4,581	1931	33	1,841
1920	65	3,718	1932	33	1.841
1921	65	3,711	1933	23	1,284
1922	63	3,625	1934	17	971
1923	53	3,025	1935	-	-
1924	53	3,023			
OIL POWERED RAIL CARS					
1934	4	201			

The Trailers

The success of the steam rail motor introduction led to several problems, not least of which was a requirement for additional accommodation within the rail motor. As this could not be achieved, the solution was a towed additional vehicle.

The construction of the early rail motors, with their match-boarded, flat-sided design, was continued with the trailer cars, although twenty-six of the former were running before the first trailer was built. The first rail motors, as can be seen from plates 18 and 19, were Nos 1 and 2 and were flat ended, but all trailers except one were built to the bow-ended format, only the first trailer having the rail motor's flat-ended format, with the match-boarded sides. Such was the demand for trailers that in 1906 existing selected coaching stock was introduced to the conversion programme. Conversion was applied to six 1890s clerestory and two four-wheelers dating back to the 1870s, the 1870s–1900s supplying some of the first conversions, with demand increasing and later periods supplying more examples for conversion, each with varying seating patterns and internal format. Thus the two four-wheel, 28.5ft-long 1870 versions were running with the new 70ft latest additions to the fleet.

We have discussed how the steam rail motor was being outclassed by demand occasioned by its own success, and the emerging 'auto train' was showing its usefulness and adaptability. Thus we find that from 1915 the steam rail motors themselves were on the downward path to becoming trailers, and a serious conversion programme was initiated. These were dealt with year by year in varying sized batches, not strictly in order of age, but the match-boarded designs preceded those of wood-panel format, and it will be noted that conversions were not applied to all rail motors and nor were such activities an annual event.

Conversions followed a similar pattern throughout the programme: the power-unit end of the cars, after quite extensive rebuilding, became the luggage compartment while the 'tail end' vestibule became the trailer driver's compartment with controls for regulator and brakes connected through to the tank locomotive, suitably modified.

Several designs of four-wheel bogie were available to supply the wheels under the original engine end of the car. To accommodate this, the underframe of the car also had to be modified to suit its new non-powered role and to conform to ordinary carriage requirements.

Developments and Missed Opportunity?

Although really not associated with the GW steam rail motor scene, and at a period, the early 1930s, when the GWR was in the last stages of phasing out its steam rail motor fleet, other developments gave a completely different slant to the rail motor question.

The Sentinel Company (Alley & MacLellan), makers of steam-driven road and rail vehicles from 1880, called a meeting in 1930 to which were invited ninety-seven company directors, managers and engineers from all over the railway world to examine and ride in a steam rail motor prior to production.

While not relevant to the GWR, did Sentinel (and other) developments of this period signal a way forward for the steam rail motor which the GWR had missed as a development opportunity? Is there still potential in such designs?

Such developments, often associated with French railways, included the use of the Woolnough marine-type boiler with superb steaming capacity, under-hung engines of up to six horizontal cylinders, both simple and compound units, oil-bath chain or Cardan shaft drives to geared axles, both coal or oil firing with automatic stokers, and flash steam boilers of various designs. A French steam railcar Sentinel Special boiler of 1935 carried a pressure of 1,300psi with Doble two-cylinder engines integral with a drive axle and pair of wheels. Such designs and thinking behind the features make the GWR steam rail motor engine unit and boiler appear positively archaic. (See plate 63 for comparison of Sentinel, GWR and Cochran boilers.) Early on in this book it is mentioned that the steam rail motor was the forerunner of the latest diesel multiple unit of three cars. A Sentinel three-car set with the above mentioned steam features is detailed in Chapter 1.

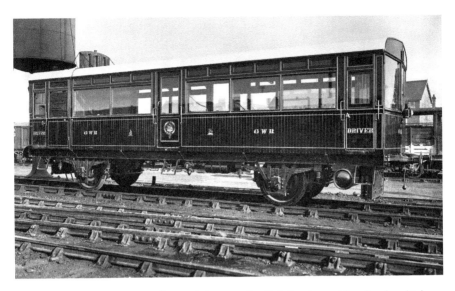

Rail motor No. 100. Its petrol/electric design was the first step toward the diesel multiple units, still some years in the future. (Steam Picture Library)

Engine and generator in GWR rail motor car, petrol/electric No. 100. (Steam Picture Library)

The control apparatus of petrol/electric rail car No. 100. (Steam Picture Library)

Great Western steam rail motor No. 15, built by Kerr, Stewart & Co with a transverse horizontal boiler. Sold to Nidd Valley Light Railway during 1920. An odd initial purchase, not to GWR design. (Steam Picture Library)

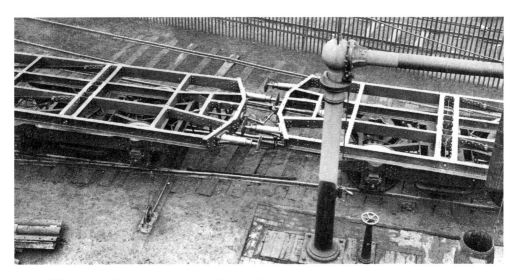

GWR steam rail motor underframes. (Steam Picture Library)

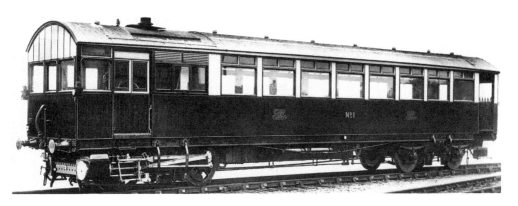

The Great Western's No. 1 rail motor. (Steam Picture Library)

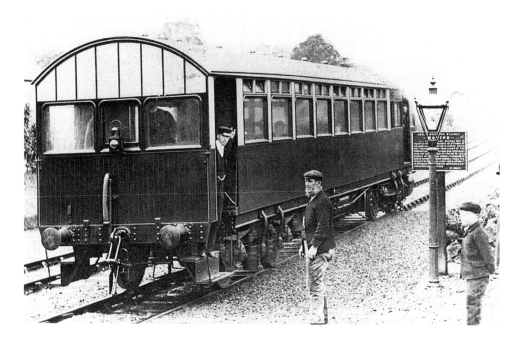

No. 1 steam rail motor including inside view. (Steam Picture Library)

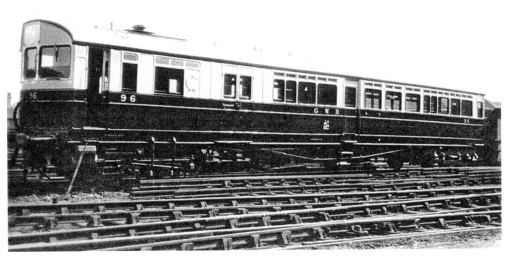

No. 96 as new and of the same batch as No. 93, the subject of the rebuild programme.

No. 45.

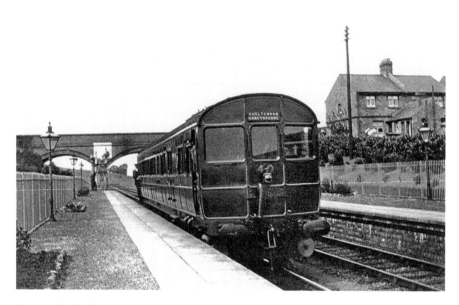

No. 40, Cheltenham to Honeybourne. This new line was introduced in 1903 to tap the fruit and vegetable potential of the Vale of Evesham. (GWR STEAM Museum, Swindon)

A GW 48XX Class locomotive.

No. 847 with a steam rail motor as a trailer.

No. 562 with two slab-sided cars, match-boarded LOT 1055, 1904. (GWR STEAM Museum, Swindon)

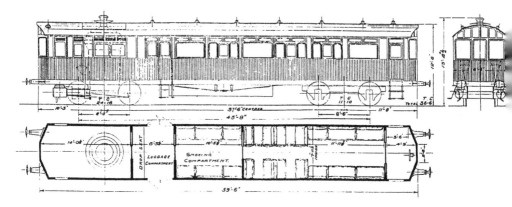

Steam motor carriage LOT 1063, Nos 19–24, 26 and 28.

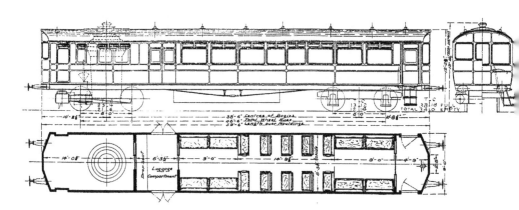

Steam motor carriage LOT 1078, No. 32.

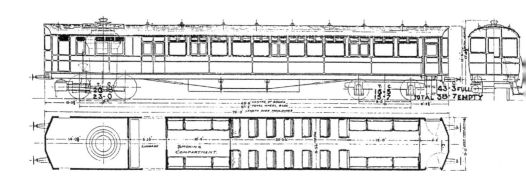

Steam motor carriage LOT 1078, Nos 38–40.

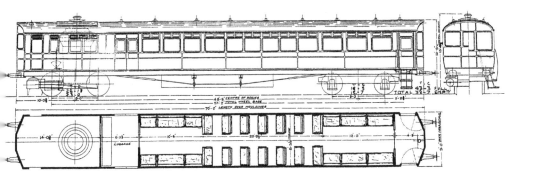

Steam motor carriage LOT 1078, No. 37.

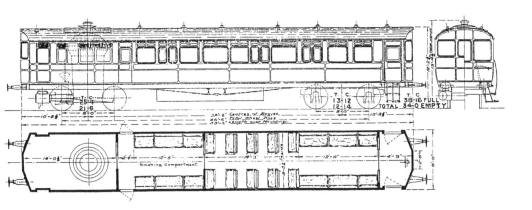

Steam motor carriage LOT 1079, Nos 41 and 42.

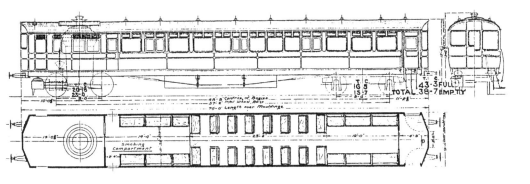

Steam motor carriage LOT 1079, Nos 44–48.

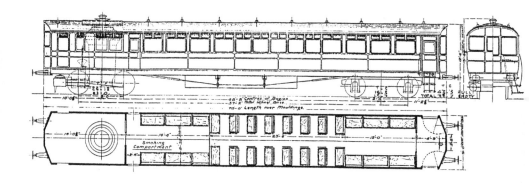

Steam motor carriage LOT 1079, No. 43.

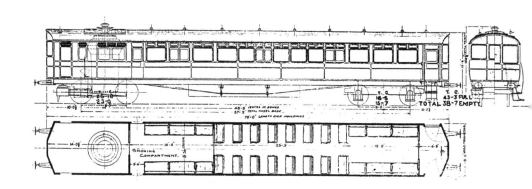

Steam motor carriage LOT 1079, Nos 49–52.

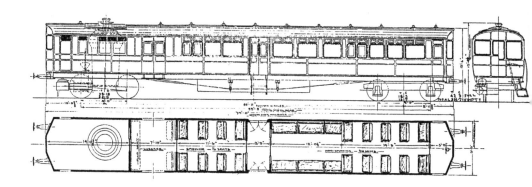

Steam motor carriage LOT 1088, Nos 53–58 and 61–72.

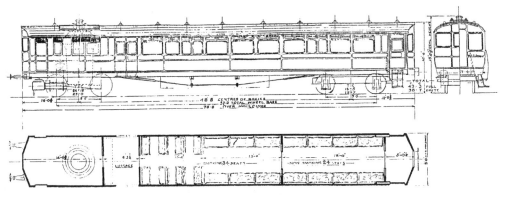

Steam motor carriage LOT 1089, Nos 59 and 60.

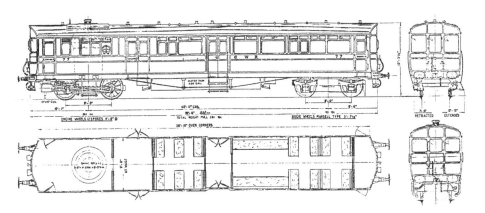

Steam motor carriage LOT 1101, Nos 73–80.

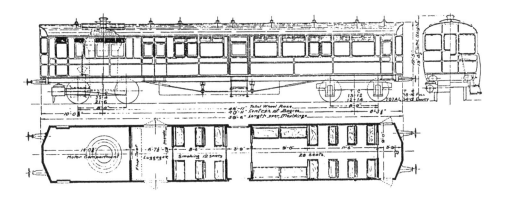

Steam motor carriage LOT 1129, Nos 81–83.

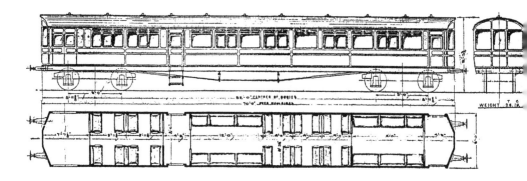

GWR Swindon trailer carriage LOT 1087, No. 15, November 1905.

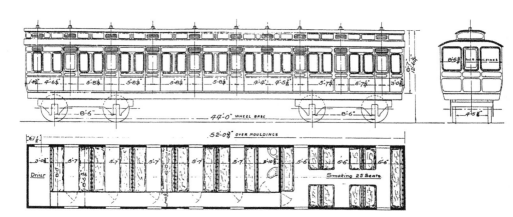

GWR Swindon trailer carriage LOT 1087, Nos 16 and 17, October 1905.

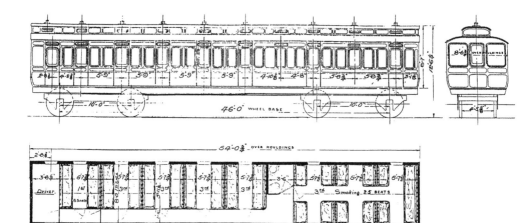

GWR Swindon trailer carriage LOT 1087, No. 18, October 1905.

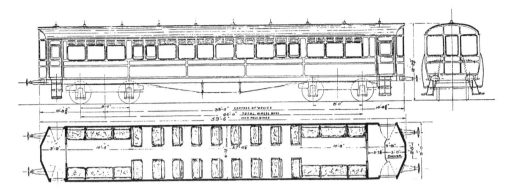

GWR Swindon trailer carriage LOT 1102, Nos 19–22, July 1905.

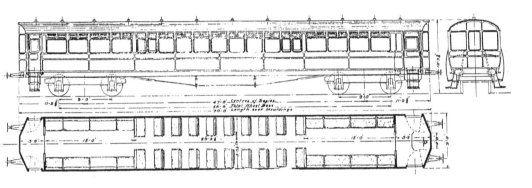

GWR Swindon trailer carriage LOT 1103, No. 28, December 1905.

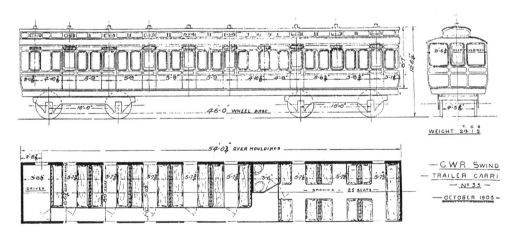

GWR Swindon trailer carriage LOT 1102, No. 35, October 1905.

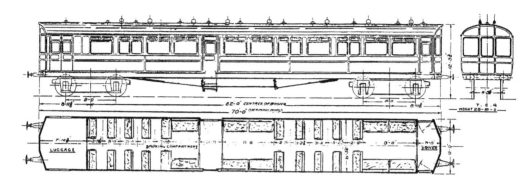

GWR Swindon trailer carriage LOT 1130, Nos 49–52.

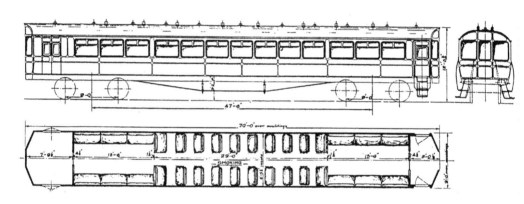

GWR Swindon trailer carriage LOT 1161, Nos 73 and 74.

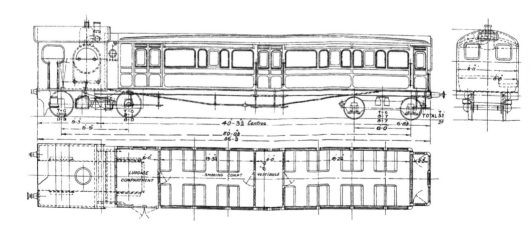

Engine 2120 – auto engine lowered with coach/body, type 3 0.6TO: Built in 1903, Lot R3 was an attempt to hide the power unit. This was not popular with operating and maintenance staff, being hot on the footplate and restricted for maintenance, but it blended with the unit contours. (Steam Picture Library)

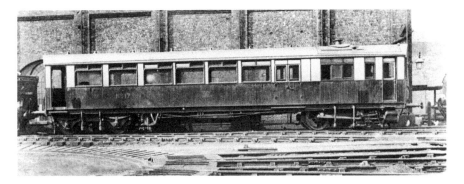

No. 17: an early flat-sided car.

Opposite bottom: Nos 15 and 16, allocated diagram E: Built by Kerr, Stuart & Co, this is a rather odd design and nothing like its fellows built to the Great Western pattern. The boiler is of locomotive type mounted transversely across the motor compartment. The 2-2-0 format of drive with only one pair actually driven from the cylinders showed a lack of power for its 56ft 3in length. The design was restricted in its practical use and the two examples were put up for sale. Only one sold, No. 15, to the Nidd Valley Light Railway in 1920 while No. 16 remained unsold and was broken up in 1927. Although built in 1904/5 they were not really a success, No. 15 clocking up less than 90,000 miles. What prompted the purchase in the first place is not known.

No. 74: an early flat-sided car with the curved coach body shape. Towing trucks: the SRM was not really suitable for shunting and was restricted in the loads it could pull.

A GWR steam rail motor power unit. The boiler design makes for interesting comparison. (Steam Picture Library)

No. 73: the problem
of removing the boiler.
Here a special frame and
block are used.

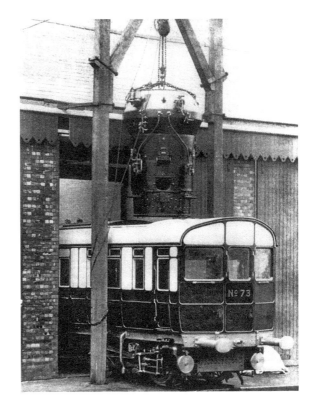

The construction of
steam rail motors:
arrangement of steam
motor – sectional
elevation.

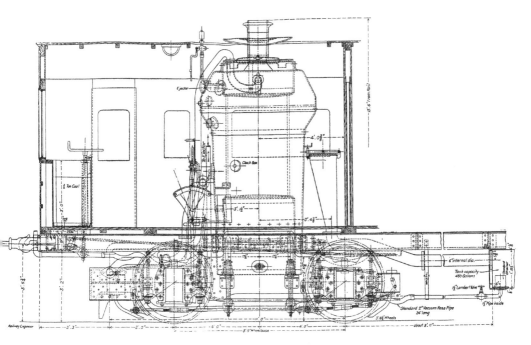

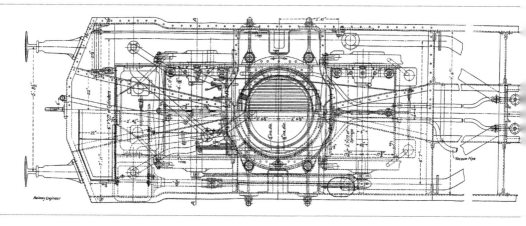

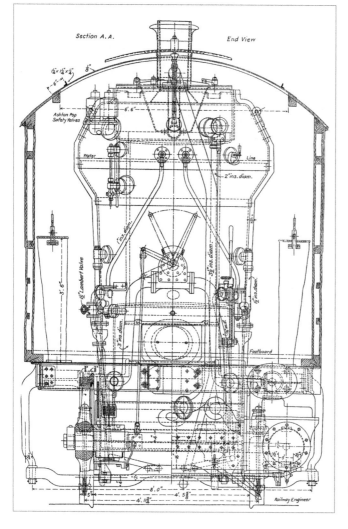

The construction of steam rail motors: arrangement of steam motor – plan.

The construction of steam rail motors: end view of cross section.

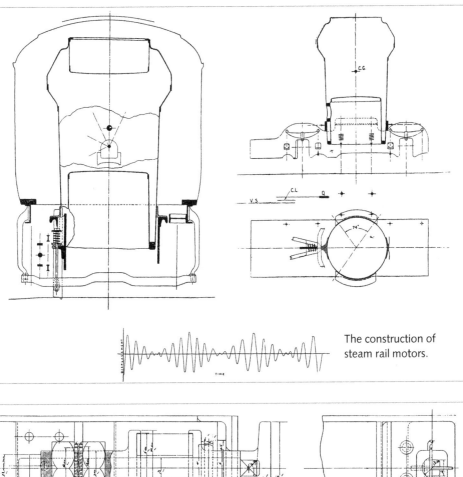

The construction of
steam rail motors.

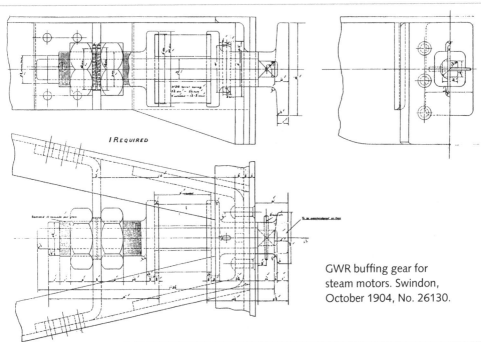

GWR buffing gear for
steam motors. Swindon,
October 1904, No. 26130.

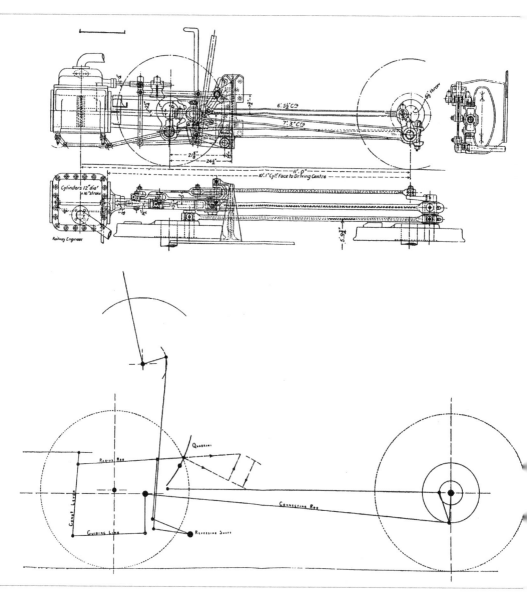

The construction of steam rail motors: arrangement of valve gear.

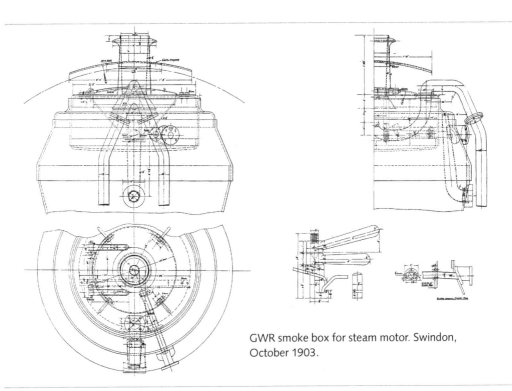

GWR smoke box for steam motor. Swindon, October 1903.

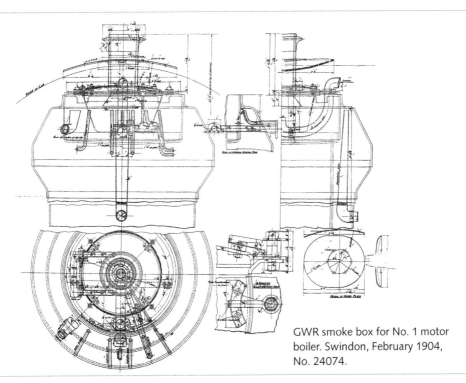

GWR smoke box for No. 1 motor boiler. Swindon, February 1904, No. 24074.

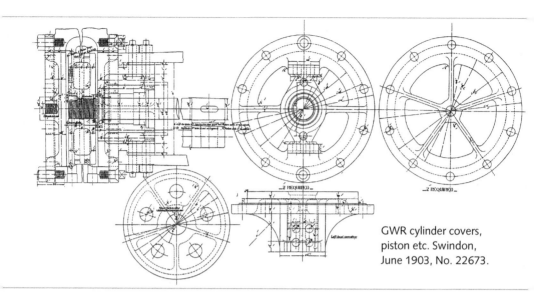

GWR cylinder covers, piston etc. Swindon, June 1903, No. 22673.

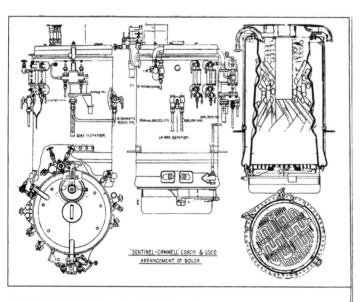

Drawing of a Sentinel boiler. Reproduced from the L&NER magazine.

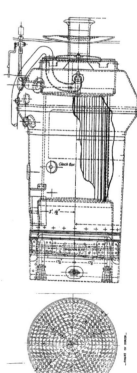

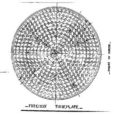

GWR arrangement of tubes for No. 1 steam motor. Swindon, February 1905, No. 26942. The GWR design has vertical fire tubes, meaning that opposite ends of the tubes are above the water line for about 6 inches, which can cause them to leak at the tube plate. The Sentinel has water filled tubes surrounded by the fire heat.

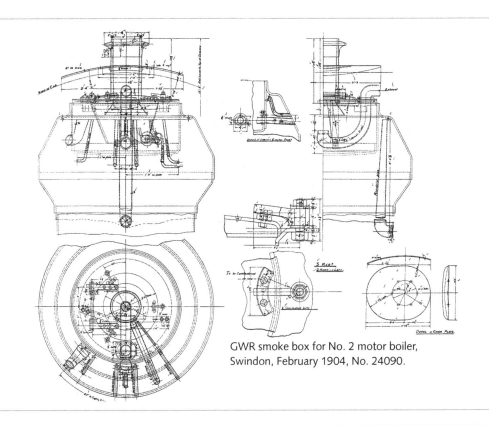

GWR smoke box for No. 2 motor boiler, Swindon, February 1904, No. 24090.

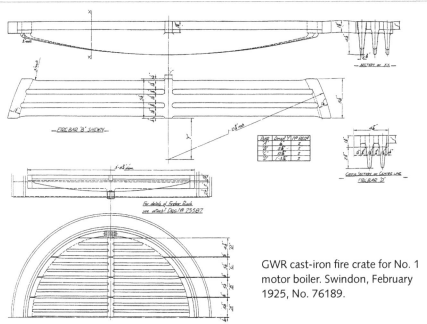

GWR cast-iron fire crate for No. 1 motor boiler. Swindon, February 1925, No. 76189.

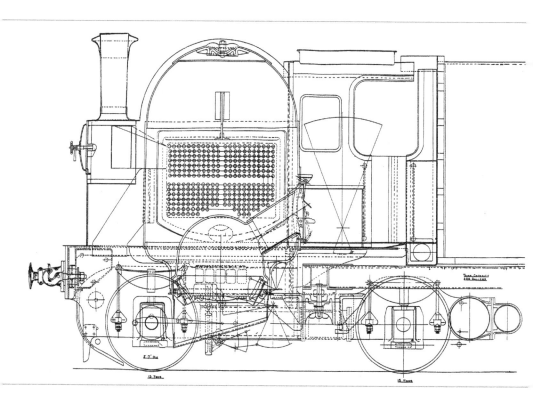

Cochran patent boiler for proposed steam motor carriage.

A Great Western Steam Rail Motor Enigma!

A Firing Experiment

While searching through the drawings from the STEAM Museum archives at Swindon, I came across Drawing No. 27390, like its fellows rather brittle and the worse for wear, dated 1904. The drawing, reproduced on the following pages, shows a design for the burner for liquid fuel applied to the boiler of a steam rail motor. While the drawing stated 'one to be fitted for trial', I had not found any reference to this in the minutes of the superintendent's meetings where all aspects of the rail motors were discussed. Several sources were also examined, including the quite detailed publication of the 'Railway Correspondence and Travel Society, Part 11, of Locomotives of the GWR' which includes 'Rail motor Information, a comprehensive listing'. Digging further, the only, and rather fleeting, reference came from *The Locomotive* magazine of 15 May 1905, page 76 and reads:

Great Western Railway: The boiler of N° 10 steam rail motor coach has been fitted with Mr Holden's apparatus for burning liquid fuel. This arrangement will not interfere with coal firing when found desirable.

The latter statement is certainly interesting! The drawing shows the apparatus apparently poking its nozzle through the firehole door horizontally as in a normal oil-fired boiler with horizontal tubes. How this would function with the vertical tubes of a rail motor boiler is not recorded (at least so far I have not been able to find out how it worked, or indeed if the Drawing No. 27390 is actually for Mr Holder's apparatus or a variation of same). The oil, or liquid fuel, is also not specified. I can see no steam pipe or pressure arrangement of any kind to spray the fuel into the firebox. The spray injector appears to be separately hinged, perhaps being capable of swinging back out of the way of the firehole door proper. James Holden was the Locomotive Superintendent of the Great Eastern Railway between the years 1885 and 1907, having spent about twenty years with the GWR at Swindon. During the early 1880s, a pollution controversy arose between the Great Eastern and local authorities, as the former was discharging residue from its oil-gas plant at Stratford into the River Channelsea. As the oil-gas was a continuing requirement at the time for lighting Great Eastern coaching stock, Holden improved an existing design of burner for his locomotives to (a) use the residue and (b) keep the authorities quiet! An ordinary locomotive firebox had the fire lit in the usual way. When the pressure reached about 30psi, broken fire brick was spread over the fire bed, to form an inert seal to the bars. Operating the control valve caused the oil burner to spray fuel into the box, the mist igniting on contact with flames from wood thrown onto the fire bed. Oil was preheated in the tank by exhaust from the Westinghouse pump. The Holden oil-burning apparatus was very successful, being applied to many locomotives on the Great Eastern. Spiralling costs and progress ended its economic use when coal gas became more readily available for carriage illumination, so the oil source dried up.

To return to the GWR and the steam rail motors, the idea of sprayed burning oil and a wood-constructed vehicle would certainly not pass the health and safety restrictions of today. Referring then to the GWR application there is a reference on the general arrangement drawing to Drawing No. 11013, which gives 'details of the injector', so some questions could have been answered. Unfortunately, after the intervening years from 1904, there is no trace of this drawing, so it looks as though the questions will remain unanswered.

A further interesting fact relating to Drawing No. 11013 is that its numbering sequence lies within drawings related to boilers for steam cranes dated within the mid–1890s period. Was the injector tried on a steam crane boiler? Yet another unanswered question.

A further technical note on the use of oil as fuel

A low-viscosity oil, such as gas oil used in the normal range of atmospheric temperatures, does not require a heater to reduce viscosity before reaching the burners (assuming it was gas-oil the GWR experiment was to use).

During this period gas-oil costs were higher than those of crude oils of higher viscosity, but not requiring a heater was a big advantage. With locomotives, a small fire was maintained in the firebox to ensure an ignition source for the oil, but this may have proved difficult on the firebrick-covered bed of the comparatively small circular firebox of a rail motor. It should be noted that the Holden system used the *residue* of a process, not 'pure' gas-oil. Control of air was a factor, and in this respect the production of smoke of a light grey colour was the best indicator of correct combustion. This produced its own problem, in that with a locomotive looking through the spectacle plate cab windows was easy, but with a steam rail motor the chimney was screened by the driving compartment roof (above the driver's head).

All in all, it was not a satisfactory rail motor system and it appears that no details of its success, or otherwise, were recorded, so, assuming it actually took place, it probably didn't last long, and whether it burnt residue or pure oil is not known.

I could find no record in the regular meeting minutes of superintendents etc., where all facets of rail motor operation were discussed, or any reference to No. 10 or oil-burning arrangements. Number 10 car was completed during May 1904 with engine unit 0812, and fitted with the oily residue burning apparatus in 1905. Number 10 itself was withdrawn in December 1916, but the engine lived on in car No. 41, which was withdrawn in September 1922, most probably finishing its days as a coal burner.

There was a major move during the early years of the twentieth century to convert the Royal Navy ships to oil burning, so it is possible that an oil-burning steam railcar was considered the height of modern technology.

There is no record that I can find of the system being abandoned. No other rail motor was so fitted, so we can only assume the experiment failed, and Mr Holden's apparatus was quietly removed.

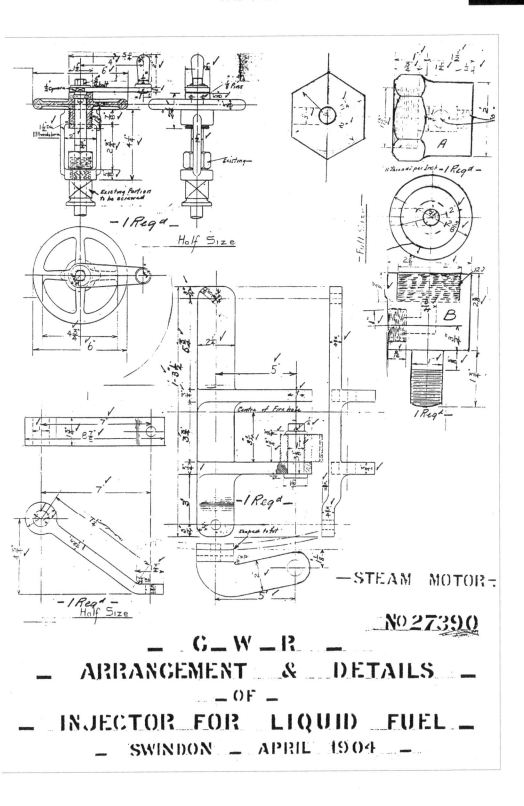

—STEAM MOTOR—

№27390

_ G_W_R _

_ ARRANGEMENT & DETAILS _

_ OF _

_ INJECTOR FOR LIQUID FUEL _

_ SWINDON _ APRIL 1904 _

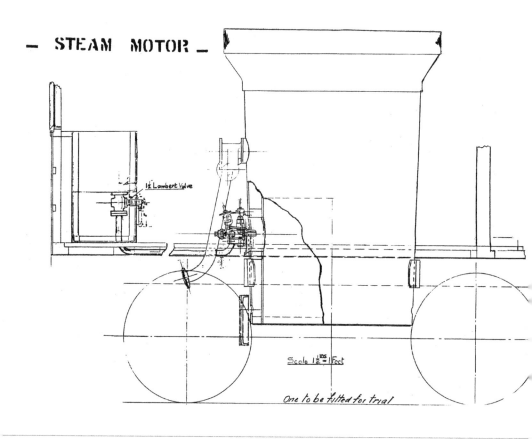

As an interesting speculation, there were several (non-GWR) designs of steam rail motor which followed the horizontal locomotive style of boiler. With horizontal fire tubes or even a water tube design (bordering on 'flash steam') would Holden's apparatus have been successful with such an application, even to the extent of application to the 'Cochran' design of boiler shown on page 70? It would have required a major cab design, but would it have worked?

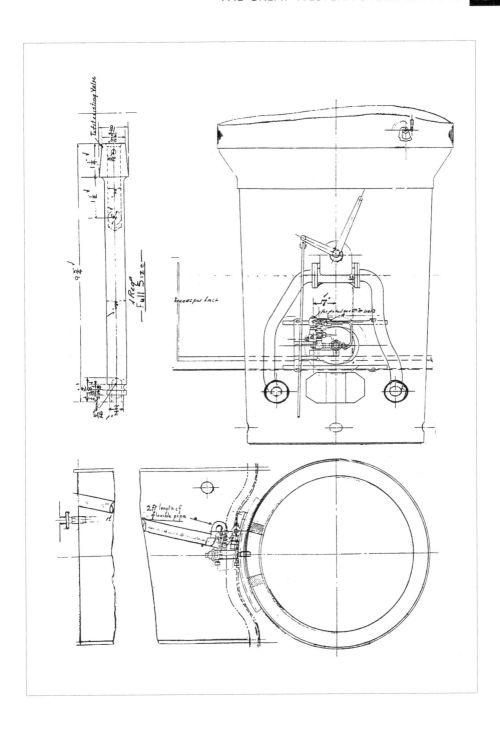

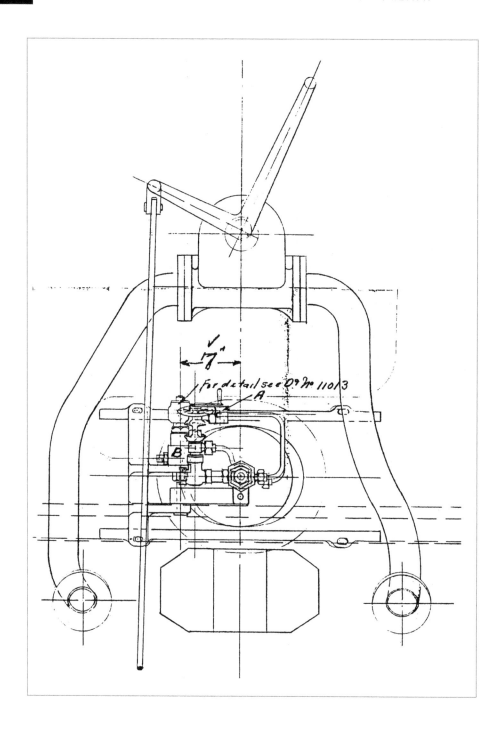

3

STEAM RAIL MOTOR DESIGN

The Engine

This hybrid vehicle exhibits the principles of both locomotive and carriage combined in a rather unique way. A locomotive-type car, the whole car up to 70 feet long, encases the complete boiler and control section of the 'engine', which swivels on four wheels under one end of the coach, while the other end is supported by a carriage-type four-wheel bogie, the latter being Dean, Standard or American type.

The power bogie was an adaptation of a Dean Suspension type, specially modified for its new role of carrying the weight of the boiler. The boiler of the rail motor acted as the centre pivot pin of the unit with specially positioned 'rubbing plates' on the sides, back and front, which located against other mating plates on the underframe. The front and back plates in this case were spring loaded to reduce any slackness (see Plate 55) and could be adjusted as required. Wheel diameters of the power unit varied with design (see table in Chapter 2) from 3ft 5½in to 4ft, the engine unit weight of the 4ft version being 8½ tons.

To allow for curves, the bogie could swivel about five degrees to the left or right, giving about 8in of movement either way. A permitted lateral movement of ¾in was also inbuilt. Very heavy cross-girders mounted at the ends of equally robust scroll irons carried the motor end of the car, the scroll irons solidly riveted to the car underframe.

Carrying the carriage load on the bogie was damped by the use of eight springs, and it was to these springs that the problems of vibration when running were attributed. Various designs of spring have different 'vibration' periods when under load, and the combination of leaf and spiral springs – four of each in this case – was thought to be the problem. Couple the spring problem (which does not appear to have been resolved) with the battering effect of a loose or maladjusted buffing spring in the boiler rubbing-plate assemblies and the vibration problems were multiplied, making for a rather uncomfortable ride.

The vertical boiler design, (tested to 220psi; working pressure 160psi) once introduced to the Great Western rail motors, was virtually standard throughout the whole period of its existence. There was an attempt to introduce oil firing, but the life of the boiler continued with very few modifications of any sort. The only major modification was the trial with variations of tube diameter relating to the heating surface total figure. As noted in the 'Problems and Failures' section later, problems were experienced regularly with leaking tubes, always dreaded by firemen, but with a vertical boiler the normal water line gave about 5 inches of tube end above the water level and into the steam space. While this probably gave a tendency toward 'drying' the steam, it certainly did not do much for the integrity of the beaded-over tube ends, top and bottom, in the tube plates. Bad scaling of the tubes was overcome by introducing a deflector at the feed point. A spring-loaded 6-ton weight of boiler, swaying in motion and with points, branch-line riding and irregularities of track with which to contend, gave a rather unstable effect to the whole. A further problem, as listed, was the leaking of the main steam pipes, so, with one pipe flange on a secured cylinder and the other on a swaying boiler, something had to give; although the engine unit, complete, was independent of the coach body. In construction, it was important to ensure that the heavy scroll irons (see plate 2) were not only securely riveted to the underframe but with critical positioning, lying on an exact circle periphery with its centre on the boiler centre, otherwise severe straining of the frame on curves would result.

The engine bogie frame was $7/8$in steel plate, and an essential consideration when building was the integrity of the rivets, as the vibrations previously mentioned soon found a rivet not closed securely and rapidly worked it loose, thus affecting others. A proposal to increase the frame thickness to 1in was considered not necessary as long as the riveting was effective. The bogie was of much heavier design generally than the normal carriage-carrying bogie. The 12in bore x 16in stroke cylinders were bolted to the mainframes and positioned 1in below the centreline of the wheels. The cylinder block casting was complicated by an integral box-like distance piece where the casting bolted to the frame, (see plate 102 for an illustration of a cylinder casting) and thus made for an equally complicated pattern requiring the equivalent of sixteen core boxes to make the various apertures.

Whalschaert valve gear operating Richardson-type balanced slide valves distributed the steam, giving easy maintenance of the gear, all being outside the frame, and good steam distribution with constant lead. The lead was $1/8$in with $4\frac{1}{2}$in valve travel, and the steam lap was $1\frac{1}{8}$in. A positive exhaust lap of $1/16$in was included, the steam lap giving crisper admission and exhaust, and increased port opening during the cycle. This in turn led to economies in steam and hence coal used.

There was a price to pay for the advantages, however, with increased wear and tear on valve and valve gear. The long travel, increasing the angularity of the quadrant, transmitted to the valve rod causing the latter to fracture on several occasions (see later section – Failure List).

A redesign of steam chest was also in use on later rail motors, as shown on the original 1903 drawing and later on a 1905 version with 4ft-diameter wheels, plus an alteration to the valve gear, which in the earlier versions had been offset, in the vertical plane, by as much as 5in. The new version had the valve spindle in line with the combination lever and the problem valve rods were almost eliminated. The original 1903 steam chest had the live steam inlet on a raised portion on top and to one side of the chest. The new 1905 design included an inlet horizontally through the bogie frame, and the chest top was without the raised portion and inlet flange.

An early problem with the Richardson balanced valve was the use of gunmetal strips, which wore very quickly and were substituted by more durable cast-iron versions. The design of the valve included a small hole in the back, with access to the exhaust port, to allow any steam that leaked past the strips to escape, but this hole was sometimes plugged to stop steam wastage. The plugging had the effect of negating the balancing effect, thus increasing pressure on the valve back, and wear on its face, and such unofficial modifications were soon stamped on.

Very detailed specifications covered the ferrous and non-ferrous metals used, as well as the production of the raw materials. For example, certain components were specified as 'open hearth' or Besemer acid steel for angles, channel and tees – Siemens-Martin steel boiler plates and acid steel (open hearth) for axles and also laminated springs. Very detailed composition specifications were set out for the non-ferrous 'yellow' metals. All materials were to be subjected to vigorous and very detailed testing procedures for tensile and elongation figures.

The spiral, conical and volute springs were also subjected to very detailed specifications and testing. A coil spring, for example, in unloaded state had to be within plus or minus $1/8$in of the specified height, otherwise it was to be rejected. Each spring had to be 'scragged' or 'brought down to its full range of five times in succession under a steam press, remaining closely compressed while it is measured…'. Laminated springs were also subjected to similar vigorous tests.

In plates 63 and 66 we saw construction details and comparisons of three rail motor boilers, all of a vertical format. At this early-twentieth-century period, and indeed up to the 1930s, there were also road vehicles and 'wagons' powered by a steam engine, engines which had varying types of steam generator ranging from 'fire tube' through 'water tube' on to the later 'flash steam' (much favoured by model engineers who were model power boat enthusiasts). The large steam wagons hauling trailers loaded with tree trunks are remembered from the 1930s by the author, the loads heading for the local timber yard and saw mill. On a smaller scale, many readers will remember the 'Stanley' steam car, and a Sentinel using a boiler designed by the American, Abner Doble. The car could have steam raised reputedly in ninety seconds!

An early design by Straker was a forerunner of the Sentinel and another fire-tube design by Robertson. Sentinel also used a water tube design by Woolnough.

On reflection, it seems the GWR should have updated their boiler design, but the seemingly rather rapid disillusion with the steam rail motor retarded any enthusiasm to proceed with redesign.

The Car Body and Frame

The body of the car was of typical period wood construction from sole bar to roof. In the early 1940s, when the author was an office boy in an office in a corner of No. 4 Coach Body Shop at Swindon Works, the only apparent difference in construction was the use of soft 'black iron' sheets in place of the wood boarding attached to the frame construction. A pervading smell in the shop, never forgotten, was the use of tallow into which all screws were dipped before being inserted in their thousands around the panels! Screwed iron sheets had been applied to rail motors to replace the match-wood boarding originally used externally.

The wood construction also precluded the suggestion made to ease the problem of lifting the boiler out vertically from the engine compartment, a high lift of some 23 feet. Some consideration was given to the removal of the boiler sideways, only a small clearance lift being required before removal, but this would have meant removable panels cutting through the coach bodywork. The idea was rejected as the cant rail and roof sticks would have to be cut through, thus 'severely weakening the end structure of the coach'. It would appear that reinforcing such an opening with the obvious steel frame was not considered, so a practical idea was dropped, and the high-lift problem continued.

The selection of woods available for car No. 1 as an example is in somewhat different mode to that of current materials when everything would probably be glossy plastic internally and very crinkled steel panels externally, the latter unacceptable in GWR days! The 32ft length of the passenger compartment was finished in polished oak, as were the seat divisions and the armrests, all topped by a white painted roof lined in blue. Baltic and Canadian oak formed the structural frame, while externally the top section was Honduras mahogany, with narrow matching, American style, for the lower half.

Accommodation for the 'strap hangers' was not forgotten; just like the London Underground, brass rails with leather hand loops attached were suspended from the roof close above the seats which were covered woven wire faced with plaited rattan cane.

From the beginning all cars were gas lit, each fitting of '14 candle power' (the strength increased to 20 candle power later on). The gas source depended on supply from tanks suspended under the car body. The gas was oil gas compressed to 140psi, with governors and pressure gauges. When some of the later cars were 'contracted out', a very detailed specification accompanied the order. Among the precise details were those for the most extensive hand-painted finish to the coach body. One such contract reads:

> The interior of the roof is to have one coat of priming, two coats of white, and one coat of perline and the mouldings picked out in blue. The sides and ends of the car must be properly cleaned off and given two coats of lead colour, four coats of filling, then rubbed down, one coat of lead colour and faced. One coat of lead colour, one coat of chocolate brown and a second coat of half varnish, half colour below the light rails, and four coats of white above the rails. The mouldings are then to have two coats of brown and the whole given one coat of varnish. The round of mouldings are then to have two coats of gold colour finished with three coats of varnish flattened down after the first coat. The inside of the car below roof is to be oak grained.

When progress had dictated soft iron sheets in place of the wood exterior, the panels were punched and countersunk at the same time around the periphery for the thousands of screws previously mentioned. On painting, each individual countersunk screw had to be filled and rubbed down to give the regular, high-gloss sheen to the finished paint. The sheets were, incidentally, not galvanised or zinc coated, and just had a blue/black surface unprotected.

It is surprising, in the current rush of industry and development, to find construction drawings and copies of drawings, almost a century old, still surviving. I remember, during the 1960s, finding drawings of pre-1914–19 vintage still in the Workshop racks, so we benefit from the never-throw-anything-away culture of the GWR.

The following drawings and photographs will form a guide to the construction of the carriage body and frame of both the 60ft and 70ft versions of the steam rail motors of the GWR. The drawings have been 'cleaned up' as copies, the originals showing the dirt, tears and repairs, torn creases etc. (the latter 'transparent' repairs now opaque and obscuring parts of the drawing) and often a missing section at the unrolling end. If left on the original drawings, the detail would be too small to read when fitted into book form.

From three-quarters of a century on from the demise of the steam rail motor, we can still see how they were built. Particular attention was to be given to the external roof, as specified:

> The roof boards, after the joints have been levelled, must be well puttied, painted (primer ?) and given a coat of thick white lead paint. Stout canvas of good quality must then be strained over and held in position by a suitable cornice screwed to the cant rails. The canvas must then be given four coats of thick white lead paint.

Construction of the car body framework was also specified in great detail. Positions of half-lap and mortised joints were clearly specified, as well as the positioning of wrought-iron reinforcing plates, elbows and brackets between frame members, securely bolted and screwed into the woodwork. As with the metalwork for the engine, quality specifications for all woodwork were to be strictly followed – seasoned, straight grained, free from knots and shakes etc. There are various methods of cutting trunks to obtain the different qualities of wood. Cheaper cutting methods produce more wood from a given baulk, but these are of lower strength due to grain formation in the cut pieces. The best quality woods are 'quarter sawn' giving less output from a given baulk but of far better quality regarding grain. Obtaining quality seasoned wood was not a problem in those early years. Natural seasoning and time taken before use was vastly different from the rapidly kiln dried, cheaply cut timber of the present day, which warps as soon as you've used it!

The rail motors demanded nothing but the best, in true GWR tradition. As an office boy in the early 1940s I remember rapidly diminishing (due to the War) acres of stocked cut wood outside the main saw mill at Swindon Works – all now long gone as well as its reason for being there!

A Note on the External Plating & Variations in the Paint Finish of Coaching Stock 1903–1950s

The year the first GWR railcar was steaming its pioneer route between Chalford and Stroud, another example of new thinking was steaming its way to Penzance, probably turning heads in non-recognition and disbelief.

On this six-coach train, the traditional painting scheme of chocolate and cream had been superseded by 'dark lake', the move being possibly to simplify the painting process, or simply a proposed way of saving money.

Whatever the analysis of this experiment showed it was to be 1908 before all-brown coaches rolled from the paint shops, resplendent in white roofs and the bodies lined out in gold leaf and black. Pulled by the steam locomotive, or with its own inbuilt boiler such as those of the steam rail motor fleet, the latter now up to almost full strength, the white roof certainly didn't remain white for very long!

Again, probably cost cutting, the gold leaf was superseded by lining in yellow ochre. Two years before the 1914–18 war put a 'stop' or at best a 'slow' notice on all cosmetic painting efforts, a change was again made and crimson lake was introduced along with a reversion to gold leaf. Two years after the conflict, maybe in an attempt to remember the days before the tragedy of war, a return was made to chocolate and cream with yellow ochre lining, gold leaf was again 'out'.

Steel panelled, wood-framed coaching stock had now been introduced generally and painting on imitation wood panels ceased in 1927 and the two traditional colours of chocolate and cream were separated by a single line in yellow ochre for general stock, and a double line for the named express stock. During 1928 the London/Bristol coats-of-arms replaced the traditional 'garter' crest, with 'GWR' above, being retained until the last years of the steam rail motor, when the letters 'GWR' were placed inside a circle, and curved to fit the periphery, a device which appeared seemingly everywhere.

The surviving steam rail motor No. 93 (ex trailer 212) when in use as a mobile office is remembered as all-brown exterior, with all-black below the sole bar, and all vestige of 'crests' long ago painted out. This brown-all-over format was reintroduced just prior to the Second World War for some of the, shall we call it, non-standard or less-important carriage stock. But once again, as the war progressed the brown was applied to all stock when shopped for repair. Cream upper works again returned during 1943, but, already as a non-standard 'trailer' car, it is possible that trailer 212 (ex SRM 93) retained its all-over brown finish. As an office vehicle, long since removed from running in traffic, and having been associated with the vehicle at this time, I cannot recall a white roof. Now a static 'building', the impression was of a very dark colour roof, possibly a weather-proofing bitumastic paint of some sort, or just the usual grime that accumulated on a static vehicle. Its recent return to traffic has seen No. 93 once again in traditional hues, and as the GWR used to be.

Incidentally, the steel panelled, wood-framed stock remembered from a 1944 association with the Coach Body Shop at Swindon (No. 4 Shop),

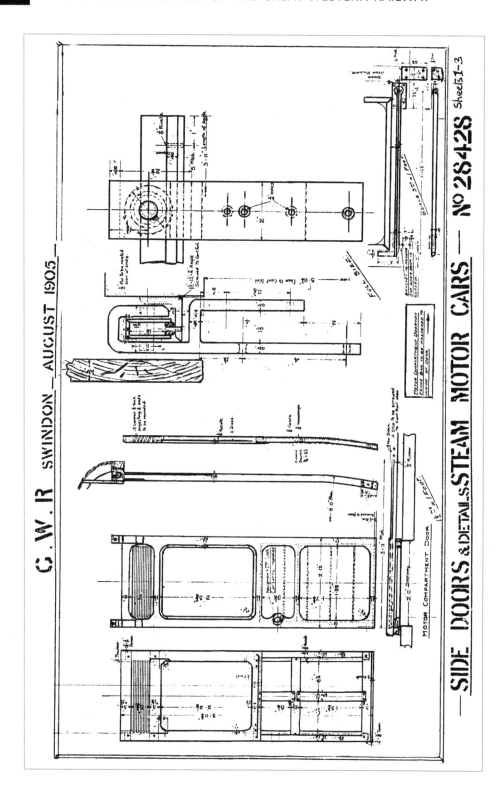

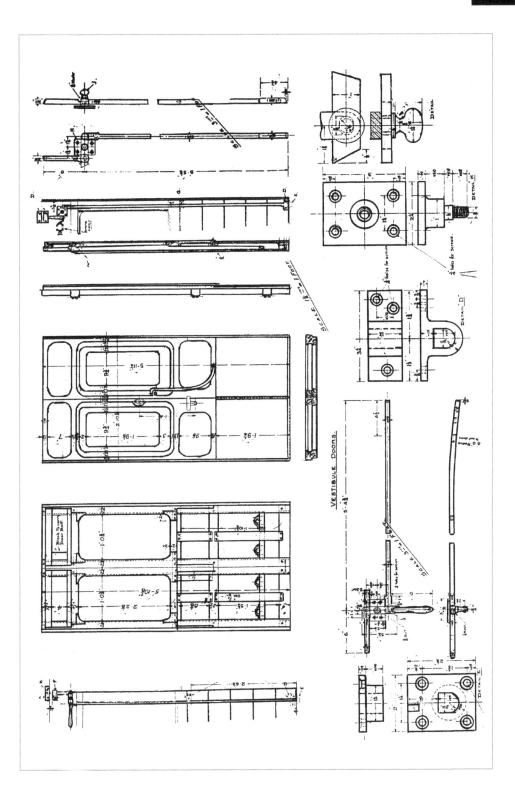

VESTIBULE DOORS.

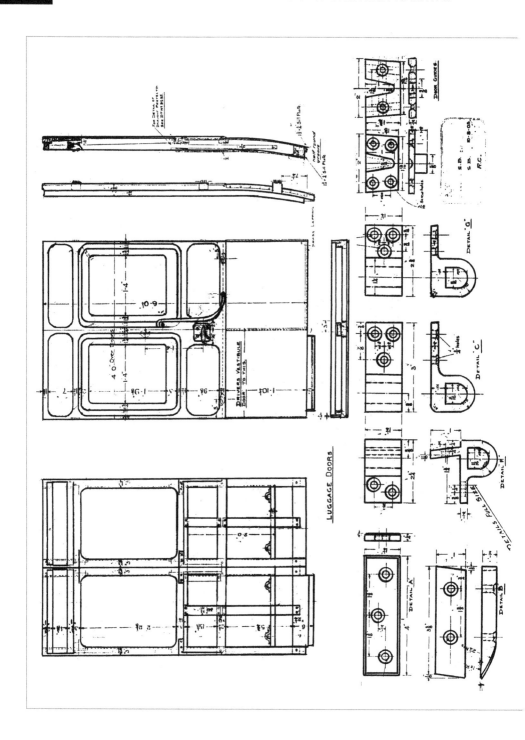

had an adjacent No. 3 Shop where all metalwork was blanked, punched and countersunk on preset presses, the myriad screw holes punched, not drilled, and press countersunk in one operation of the press. The plates were of very soft mild steel, seemingly generally referred to at the time as 'Russian's black iron', but as this period was the tail end of the Second World War such a description was probably not accurate and based on pre-war sources. On assembly the blue/black plates and shapes were assembled straight onto the wood frames, they were not galvanised, or zinc plated etc. in any way, neither were they red leaded or similar on the inside surfaces, although white lead paint may have been applied to the woodwork and the plates assembled while this was still wet, but memory may be wrong.

As already mentioned, all the screws used were dipped in tallow before insertion, and the rancid smell is a lasting memory of the Coach Body No. 4 Shop, Swindon Works. This technique was not applied to No. 93 rebuild. The number of steel, countersunk wood screws used on one coach must have numbered hundreds of thousands, and all inserted by 'belly brace' or hand screwdriver. The pre-war introduction of the American 'pump' screwdriver was apparently banned from use on the GWR for a number of years as it would have destroyed the 'piece work' price set for the other means of screw insertion, and given some staff an 'unfair advantage'. The 'productivity' aspect did not enter the equation! So much for progress and fear of change.

Problems and Failures

The concept of the steam rail motor was a good one, and it fitted well into the period into which it was introduced. The slow-moving and scattered rural communities of the early twentieth century were opened up with regular local transport facilities at set times to neighbouring towns and markets. The war of 1914–18 was to dramatically change the 'idyllic' (on paper at least) way of life.

The expansion of transport and communication introduced by the rail motor benefited the railway as a whole, before becoming itself overtaken by events of population and goods movements to an extent not envisaged on the rail motor's introduction. These benefits were somewhat negated by the various failures of the rail motors when in service, failures which caused some head scratching on the technical side, and from which patterns emerged.

These failures were to show very early in the life of the motors, with problems on the engine side of the combination recorded in some detail, such that it was recommended that spare motor units be obtained. The early problems were of a serious nature, as it was no easy task to change a complete unit, and to lift out a boiler required a lifting range of about 23ft, often requiring the services of a breakdown crane to get the height of overhead lift, a height that could not be reached in an outstation depot lifting shop with the usual fixed 50-ton hoist. The change was thus a job for one of the major works or special hoist facilities.

The monthly analysis of rail motor failures includes the type of fault, number of the car involved and, significantly, ordinary train mileage run as a result of the rail motor failure, and which the rail motors were intended to reduce. An analysis of four-month periods, September–December 1906 and January–April 1907 are included as examples, and highlight the particularly recurring faults and failures. The problems were not restricted to any particular batch, but were spread over the complete fleet. An early modification to the boiler appeared to eliminate, except for the odd occasion, the leaky problem.

As the years passed, subsequent routine superintendents' meetings became the forum for discussion and recording of steam motor failures. At the meeting of Tuesday 5 February 1907, Mr Churchward drew attention specifically to the problems of leaking tubes and broken steam pipes. From the records it is not possible to establish where the tubes actually leaked, but with a vertical, multi-tube boiler it was probably at the top tube plate (see plate 63). These tube ends and tube plates are completely above the water line, and although it was claimed the tubes were surrounded by water bubbles, they were not therefore completely submerged as in an ordinary locomotive boiler. There does not seem to be a move to radically change the design, although a 'Cochran' drawing was prepared (see plate 66), I could find no record of one having been actually fitted. Would a vertical marine-style water-tube boiler have worked? We shall now never know.

The steam pipe problem (see plate 60) was probably inherent in the necessary design. Cylinders attached to a moving bogie and a rocking vertical boiler set up inevitable problems of stresses in pipe and joint flanges, the pipes being rather long from boiler to cylinder.

By 1910 the written 'returns' concerning rail motors were reduced to eliminate recording and clerical duties as much as possible. As the Great War ground on into 1915, the meeting of 1–2 June 1915 ended with the note 'Records subsequent to this date have been temporarily suspended.' The suspension was apparently to become permanent as the steam rail motor was progressively phased out following the conflict and no more records appeared.

Another problem seemingly inherent in the design, not a 'failure' as such but certainly causing a recognisable discomfort to passengers, was the tendency of the cars to vibrate under certain circumstances. There were theories on the reason for this (given in more detail in the Design section of this book), the major vibrations occurring when the car was going downhill, engine first. The vibrations seemed to build up to a peak and then ease off. There were comments from technical staff that anyone travelling in a car with a slack 'buffing spring' would certainly know about it! This buffing arrangement was to take some of the movement shock out of the frame when running, but the 'hunting' action was certainly commented on unfavourably, and was apparently not cured fully although a change of spring design was introduced in some of the later engines.

Apart from the isolated modifications mentioned, there was to be no major updating of the railcar fleet, established solidly by 1908. The design of the power bogie did not change, and the same style of boiler was retained throughout. If an enterprising young designer had been allowed a chance, maybe, just maybe, a new design could have saved what was really a very useful concept for travel but one which was allowed to retain its problems of power and repairs and ultimately to be killed off.

Examples of Failure Details from Superintendents' Monthly Meetings

NUMBER OF TIMES OCCURRING IN VARIOUS PERIODS SHOWING A GENERAL IMPROVEMENT

THE PROBLEM	SEPT (1906)	OCT	NOV	DEC	JAN (1907)	FEB	MAR	APR	MAY	JUN	JUL	AUG	SEPT	OCT	NOV	DEC	JAN (1908)	8 WKS (1912)
WEAR & TEAR?	1	3	10	1	2		1	4		1	3			1		1	1	
LEAKY TUBES	5	3	1	1												1	1	
BROKEN SUSPENSION BOLT	1											1	1					
BROKEN BRAKE PULL ROD (OR UNCOUPLED)	1			1								1						
FIRE BARS FALLING OUT!	1	1									1							
SPRING FRACTURE OR HANGER	3																	1
REPLACE BRAKE BLOCKS	1								1									
UNABLE TO STEAM?	1					1		1										
BURST STEAM PIPE/FLANGE LIVE OR EXHAUST	1	3	3	2	2	1												1
FIREBOX LEAK	1																	
BROKEN BUFFER	2	1			1						1							
PISTON GLAND PACKING BLOW OUT	1																	
2 BURNT FIRE BARS OR DROPPED	1			2														
BROKEN SPRING HANGER / PIN	1				2		1										1	
VALVE SPINDLE BROKEN / FAILED			4	3										1			1	1

A SUMMARY OF ANNUAL TOTAL FAILURES FROM THE START OF RECORDS OCTOBER 1905 – MARCH 1915 WHEN RECORDING WAS SUSPENDED

1905 (last 3 months)	59
1906	169
1907	64
1908	40
1909	39
1910	84
1911	45
1912	33
1913	38
1914	30
1915 (first 3 months)	12

Note: The records began with details of Failures, Minutes Delay caused by the failure and total train miles caused by railcar failure. The latter was then changed to failures per miles run in total, and then to failures only.

Introduced 1903, by 1905 it was 'decided to record the traffic derived from these cars'.

From 1 July to 31 December 1905, 2,875,679 passengers were carried by railcars. Receipts were £35,719; Rail Mileage 703,695 miles. From 1 January 1906 to 7 January 1906, 128,411 passengers were carried. Receipts were £1,287 12s 9d and the Mileage 34,646. The early successes were now established.

Defect	Recorded entries (per column, left to right)
WINDOW GLASS BROKEN	1
BROKEN FIRE BAR BRACKET	1
MANHOLE JOINT BLOWN	1, 1
BRASS AND PIN MISSING	1
SET PIN WORKED OUT	1, 1
INJECTOR FAILED	1, 1, 1, 2, 2, 3
END OF BLOWER PIPE BLOWN OUT	1, 1, 1, 1
QUADRANT / VALVE DEFECTIVE	1, 1, 1, 1
DEFECTIVE SAFETY VALVE	1, 2, 2
LUBRICATOR STEAM PIPE BROKEN	1, 1
SIDE BAR BOLTS BROKEN	1
VACUUM CYLINDER FAILED	1, 1, 1
BROKEN BLOWER RING	1, 1, 1
STEPS BROKEN	1
FEED PIPES BROKEN	1
FIREHOLE DOOR LEAKING	1
REAR CYLINDER COCK BROKEN	1, 1, 1
DEFECTIVE CYLINDER / STEAM CHEST	1, 1, 1, 1
BROKEN REGULATOR	1, 1, 1
ECCENTRICS DEFECTIVE	1, 1
SAND PIPE FAILING	1
CRANK PIN BROKEN	1
REVERSING LEVER BROKEN	1
SNIFTING VALVE DEFECTIVE	1

Mishaps Maybe but Never Accidents

Following on from the Problems and Failures section, we continue in a different vein.

A director is recorded as rebuffing a questioner with: 'Accidents? On the Great Western, Sir, mishaps maybe, but never accidents!' So, whatever one may wish to call them, there were certainly incidents that affected the steam motor fleet. Some were quite trivial, but some of the more serious included personal injury to operating and other personnel, and the destruction by fire of SMR No. 48 in 1916. Selected incidents such as those following make interesting period comments, and make an addition to the clinical facts and figures of operating and technical details of the steam rail motors.

A seemingly trivial occurrence, but one which could have resulted in serious injury, occurred on 9 June 1915 when a schoolboy in SRM 56 threw away orange peel, which hit the passing driver of 1644 in the face, damaging an eye.

Slipping on steps or on the footplate was a fairly common occurrence, and there were other footplate injuries also common. Coaling strains are listed regularly, examples being car No. 2 (26 October 1903); No. 8 (18 May 1909) at Llwyneinion; No. 13 (14 April 1906); No. 14 (8 November1906); No. 28 (23 May 1916) coaling at Southall; No. 36 Dauntsey (24 August 1916); No. 40 (21 April 1911) Malvern Road, Cheltenham; No. 48 (23 November 1907) Haresfield; No. 58 (15 January 1912) coaling Newton Abbott and so on. Seemingly coaling a steam rail motor was quite a hazardous exercise when a coal stage and facilities could not be used and coal was manhandled completely.

There were a surprising number of occasions when the footplate staff actually fell out of the cab onto the platform or the ballast, some while looking for tools: No. 83 fireman fell out of the car at Fishguard on 1 March 1916; No. 92 driver fell out onto the ballast at Southall; No. 100 petrol-electric car (20 July 1914) driver fell to the ground at Slough; No. 76 fireman fell off the frames while changing lamps (20 October 1917); No. 61 driver fell back onto platform, hitting his head and died at West Ealing (21 June 1906); No. 70 (14 March 1917) driver slipped between rail motor and platform; and so on.

Equally dangerous was looking out of windows and banging heads on obstructions: No. 46 fireman hit head on post at Winchcombe (3 February 1906); No. 49 fireman hit signal ladder at Ashbarton (3 March 1905); No. 53 (20 September 1910) at Llangybi, 9:42 a.m. ex Lampeter, fireman leaned out, head hit wall; No. 95 (4 June 1913) fireman hit head leaning out of window at Halesowen; No. 47 at Ruabon (13 August 1907) fireman from another engine was crossing the line to get to the station toilet and was knocked over by No. 47; man suffered fractured skull but recovered later.

Collisions between rail motors themselves and other traffic also occurred with undesirable frequency, for example No. 13 (14 January 1913) collided with locomotive 3534 (lot 73 – 4-4-0 3521 to 3540) at Swindon. Both were damaged.

No.	DATE	EVENT
18	27/12/1912	Collided in a siding at Wrexham with No. 20.
32	16/08/1915	Damaged in collision due to ineffective lookout during shunting.
36	31/12/1904	Hit engine of passing train due to RM driver in engine room instead of in the vestibule.
37	26/02/1914	Collided with locomotive 3209 at Oxford. No. 37 was the cause of the collision – both damaged.
38	12/02/1915	Run into by 7.50 a.m. passenger train Cardiff–Birmingham.
59	12/06/1915	Hit by engine at Clevedon and badly damaged.
65	18/07/1910	Derailed at Cheltenham.
68	08/09/1910	At Stourbridge, overran the points and derailed.
70	09/12/1910	Damaged chimney at Croes Newydd shed when a 'Not to be Moved' notice board hit and damaged the smoke troughing in the shed roof.
72	16/10/1907	Collided with No. 91 at Old Hill and broke buffers.
73	20/11/1911	Hit coal truck at Evesham.
79	14/02/1909	Hit trailer No. 5 – both damaged.
83	16/08/1909	Collided with static loco 3226 and injured the driver who was leaning below, into the motion, with an oil can.
84	16/01/1909	Collided with No. 3413 at Worcester coal stack.

The foregoing thus gives an idea of some of the dangers faced by footplate staff and the steam rail motors themselves during the course of an ordinary working life. Most could be attributed to human error and not to the motors themselves, so really nothing changes in any occupation even to the present day.

4

SHEDDING FACILITIES FOR STEAM RAIL MOTORS

The introduction of the new steam rail motors also meant providing for their stabling and maintenance where, not only were small steam engines to receive attention but there was also an attached 'coach' to consider. The facilities followed the rise and fall of the rail motors' popularity, and the following lists provide the introduction and demise dates at the stabling sites. Some records are missing, some are not complete, but those listed still give considerable information and present a reliable picture.

It will be noted particularly from the data the seemingly very large percentage of steam rail motors 'out of commission' for repairs, taken as 'repair' requirements of the 'engine' as opposed to the 'carriage' sections. The numbers listed as 'under repair' and 'awaiting repair' appear to indicate the existence of rather severe problems inherent with the concept. There could be two causes for this: (a) either the manufacture of the engine section was at fault, which, knowing GWR standards, was unlikely, or (b) the design was faulty, or at least had problems inbuilt due to the very nature of requirements. This latter was more likely the case and the real fly in the ointment was in all probability the essential boiler, which, as the technical section of this book shows, had to have the required steaming capacity and thus was the unbalanced, seemingly top-heavy design installed. This put stresses on the suspension leading to all sorts of other associated problems. (The breakdown records, shown in the previous chapter, indicate boiler tube and steam pipe problems as a regular occurrence.)

From about 1917 the enthusiasm for the steam rail motor was also now under a question mark and numbers were starting to be reduced. A number were converted to 'trailers' for the 'small loco plus X number of coaches', which was now slowly covering some requirements throughout the system. Shedding and facilities for the steam rail motor presented their own peculiar problems. Maintenance of locomotives with day-to-day servicing was usually in their own running shed. Carriages were similarly dealt with in carriage sheds. The hybrid rail motor was neither one nor the other. The carriage section in a running shed had the potential to come out dirtier than when it went in. The 'engine' section couldn't be dealt with in a carriage shed, without some adaptation to the shed.

The first facilities for rail motors when introduced at Chalford in 1903 included a corrugated iron shed, which a couple of years later was completely gutted by fire. A rail motor was destroyed in the blaze, but two other vehicles were dragged clear and saved. The cause of the fire was not established. Incidentally, only two special sheds were ever built to house and service rail motors. A further problem with the rail motor was that, should either the carriage section or the engine section need attention (usually the latter), the complete unit was out of commission for the repair period. The shedding problem was raised as a question at the International Railway Congress Association, Eighth Session, at Berne, July 1910. Report number three presented at this meeting by Mr T. Hurry Riches of the Taff Vale Railway contained analyses of a number of questions relating to steam and other rail motors asked of 'Great Britain and her Colonies'. Twenty-one railway companies replied, including data from Britain, South Africa, Australia, India and Ireland. Question six on page xii of 151 reads: '(a) Do you find cars if stabled in locomotive sheds suffer deterioration in the upholstering and accessories through difficulty in keeping them in a good state of cleanliness? (b) Have they proved an encumbrance in any way at the depots?' The GWR's reply, having already stated in answer to a previous question that only two special sheds were provided for steam rail motors throughout the system, was as follows:

a) No deterioration of body of the car, upholstering etc that could be attributed to the cars stabling in the same shed as locomotives, or to the fact that the mechanical portion is attached to the car.

b) No complaint as to cleanliness. No delays or special difficulties owing to locomotive depots being used by cars.

On a further question concerning the difficulty of taking on water, the GW's reply was 'No special appliances for this purpose, same water arrangements as for locomotives'. The latter must have been a 'tongue in cheek' reply, as a rail motor attempting to use a leather bagged water column presents a rather humorous picture! The shed hose was used to fill the 450 gallon tanks under the body, and the coal was loaded from bags (capacity 1.5 tons) as conventional coaling from the coal stage overhead platform was out of the question. Humping coal bags or baskets is not conducive to an untroubled human back! In answer to a further question asked at the Congress, the GWR stated that out of their one hundred steam rail motors, an average of seventy-nine were employed daily.

The Working Life of Cars

By the beginning of the First World War, the GWR's romance with the steam rail motor was beginning to fade and in September of 1914 cars 4–8 were withdrawn to be converted to trailers, a process which was to continue until the end of the SRM in the mid 1930s. (Note: 1907, 1920 and 1933 registers of allocations are missing from the official records.)

Recording the detail of breakdown and repairs was discontinued in 1915. The number of cars 'under repair' increased throughout the duration of the conflict, due probably to staff shortages and different priorities for the workshops, and by 1918 more than half the fleet was, for several months, incarcerated at various repair depots and workshops. Conversions continued, and in 1919 still half the fleet was awaiting repair or conversion to trailers, and it was not until 1922 that the percentage of cars out of service started to drop below the 50 per cent level, but only slightly. Cars 'in store' also were on the increase.

Over the preceding decade, the withdrawal and conversion of cars to trailers had reduced the fleet itself, and this trend was to continue until the end of the SRM. Therefore, the actual number of cars under repair also fell, but the percentage out of action remained roughly the same. Some cars were awaiting repair for more than twelve months.

It should be noted that car No. 48 was destroyed by fire at Chalford in 1916 and condemned in 1918! Number 45 was transferred to Invergordon during January 1918, car No. 15 was sold to Mr J. Wake in April 1920 and car No. 42 was sold to Mr Graham of the Port of London Authority in July 1920. Car No. 100, the only IC-engined experiment, is recorded as sold September 1919, a one-off, experimental vehicle, although its 'maintenance' record was quite good.

At the end of the steam rail motor era, cars not converted were condemned and scrapped. The sole survivor was No. 93, which appears again fifty years or so after its introduction, its history listed to date, as the final chapter of this book.

On the following lists, the status and location changes is shown as follows:

A) On Shed and Working: Named shed or abbreviation followed by a tick (✓) for duration and dates if known. Or

B) Swindon or other Works under Repair: Works name or abbreviation followed by ☒ for duration and dates. Or

C) 'In Stock': Works Name or abbreviation followed by ☑ for duration and dates.

The status and location changes of individual cars follows the example shown, using the previous abbreviation list. (Fictitious example to use all information.)

Example:

Year 1111

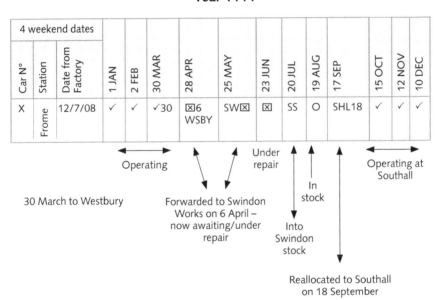

Car N°	Station	Date from Factory	1 JAN	2 FEB	30 MAR	28 APR	25 MAY	23 JUN	20 JUL	19 AUG	17 SEP	15 OCT	12 NOV	10 DEC
X	Frome	12/7/08	✓	✓	✓30	☒6 WSBY	SW☒	☒	SS	O	SHL18	✓	✓	✓

4 weekend dates

Operating

30 March to Westbury

Forwarded to Swindon Works on 6 April – now awaiting/under repair

Under repair

In stock

Into Swindon stock

Reallocated to Southall on 18 September

Operating at Southall

Note: The records from which these lists were compiled were rather 'scruffy' in the earlier years until a pattern evolved. The years 1907 into 1908 appear to be missing at the DRO, several sources being checked. Also the records for the years 1920 and 1933 have disappeared.

From the general details, it appears that the steam rail motors rarely finished the year at the shed where they were stabled at the start of the year in question. Breakdown led to replacement and so they were always on the move, repaired, into stock, re-scheduled somewhere else as a replacement to themselves. See Chapter 2 for listed details of steam rail motors to trailers.

Named Sheds or Works Locations and Abbreviations which appear on the following SRM Fleet Shed Lists

ABERDARE	ADARE	MACHYNLLETH	MLETH
ABERYSTWYTH	ABYTH	MALVERN WELLS	MWELLS
ASHBURTON	ASHB	MOOR STREET	-
BANBURY	BAN	(TYSELEY)	
BARRY	BAR		
BATH	BATH	NEATH	NTH
BRISTOL	B	NEWPORT	NPT
BLAENAVON		NEWQUAY	NEQ
BIRKENHEAD	BIRK	NEWTON ABBOT	NA
CAMBRIAN LINES	CAM LIN		
CHELTENHAM	CHELT	OLD OAK COMMON	OOC
CHIPPENHAM	CHIP	OSWESTRY	OSTY
COLEHAM	-	OXFORD	OX
CORWEN	CORWN		
CROES NEWYDD	CNYDD	PENMAENPOOL	PMNPL
		PENZANCE	PEN
DUFFRYN (INC PORT TALBOT)	DUFF	PONTYPOOL ROAD	PPRd
DIDCOT	DID		
		RADSTOCK	RAD
EBBW JUNCTION	EBBW	READING	RDG
EVESHAM	EVE		
EXETER	EX	SALTNEY	SALTY
		SLOUGH	SLGH
		SOUTHALL	SHL
GARNANT	GAR	ST PHILLIPS MARSH	StPHIM
(INC LLANELLI & GC GURWEN)		STOURBRIDGE	STOUR
GLOUCESTER	GL	SWINDON WORKS	SW
GOODWICK (INC FISHGUARD)	GCK	SWINDON STOCK	SS
		TAUNTON	TTN
		TENBY	TNBY
HALESOWEN		TROWBRIDGE	TROW
HELSTON	HEL	TRURO	TRU
		TYSELEY	TYS
KIDDERMINSTER	KIDD		
		WESTBURY	WSTY

LAMBOURN VALLEY	LAMBVAL	WEYMOUTH	WEY
LAIRA	LAIRA	WORCESTER	WOS
LLANIDLOES	LLDLS	WHITLAND (?)	WHIT
		WREXHAM	WREX
		WOLVERHAMPTON	W
		WOL STAFFORD RD	STRD
		YATTON	YAT
		YEOVIL	YVL

The Working Life of Car No. 93 (now preserved) and its Stabling Points

Number 93 was one of the last batch of rail motors constructed during 1907 at the cost of £2,100 each (today it will probably cost this for the eccentric rods alone). The rail motor entered service on 5 March 1908, stabled at Southall, where it remained for about eighteen months, operating in the Paddington–Brentford branch and West London area. With the exception of 1914–15 when it was located at Pontypool Road it remained at its new location at Stourbridge until 1917. The car then had a varied career from the end of the First World War, when the diminishing effectives of the steam rail motors were beginning to be felt. Moved to Bristol for three stints – 1917–20, 1923, and again 1929–31, it also served at Yatton, Trowbridge and Bath. Transferred to the Northern Division for 1921–22 at Croes Newydd, it worked in the Wrexham area. Also listed are sojourns at Ruabon, Gobowen, Llangollen, Delgellan and Bala. Shedded at Chalford for three years, 1924–27, it was moved to Taunton for two years working Langport to Castle Cary.

Number 93 returned to its final shed at Stourbridge, being withdrawn during November 1934 having been removed from active service on 20 May 1934. With the usual working life maintenance requirements we find that No. 93, now fitted with power unit No. 873 and boiler 1095, went into retirement and subsequent disposal. Meanwhile, the coach body, having completed almost 480,000 miles, continued as trailer car 212 into a rather uncertain future, but became a sole survivor of the fleet before eventually being withdrawn from official duties in 1956.

The following pages show the charted history of car No. 93 during its working life as a steam rail motor. It will be noted that in the early years there seems to have been a severe problem with wheels and tyres, and a continual swapping around of wheels from other cars, and this is only one rail motor out of the ninety-nine!

STEAM RAIL MOTOR CAR SHED ALLOCATIONS

CHART HISTORY OF CAR No. 93 by Ralph Tutton (SOURCE: P.R.O. RAIL 254, PIECE 66 et seq)

CAR No 93

YEAR	[DIVISION] SHED	DATE SENT FROM FACTORY												
1908	[LONDON] SOUTHALL	5.3.08	JAN 4 FEB 1 FEB 29 MAR 28 APR 25 MAY 23 JUNE 20 JULY 18 AUG 15 SEPT 12 OCT 10 NOV 7 DEC 3										COMPLETED FEBRUARY 8TH
1909	SOUTHALL	5.3.08 ×	JAN 2 JAN 30 FEB 27 MAR 27 APR 24 MAY 22 JUNE 19 JULY 17 AUG 14 SEPT 11 OCT 9 NOV 6 DEC 4					S.W.				22.11 STORE	12 days
			Stopped 29.3.09 SOUTHALL Set to work 10.4.09										77 days
			30.8.09 SWINDON 18.11.09 SW 806 BC 1046										
			13.11.09 Wheels changed L×D from Car No. 69 (0842?) and new tyre L×D										
1910	[WOLVERHMTN] STOURBRIDGE 22.11.09		JAN 1 JAN 29 FEB 26 MAR 26 APR 23 MAY 21 JUNE 18 JULY 16 AUG 13 SEPT 10 OCT 8 NOV 5 DEC 3 DEC 31										W STOVE
		×	Stopped 5.5.10 STAFFORD ROAD set to work 13.5.10 L×O 66349 BC 1093										8 days
			25.11.10 STAFFORD ROAD " 19.12.10 82107 BC 1028										24 "
			17.12.10 Wheels changed L×D from Car No 87 (0842?)										
1911	STOURBRIDGE 22.11.09		JAN 28 FEB 25 MAR 25 APR 22 MAY 20 JUNE 17 JULY 15 AUG 12 SEPT 9 OCT 7 NOV 4 DEC 2 DEC 30									SW	
			Stopped 23.3.11 STOURBRIDGE set to work 14.4.11 Staff Rd. 89620 BC 1125										22 days
			23.11.11 STAFFORD ROAD SWINDON 6.12 103 882 BC 1047										
1912	S. WORKS		JAN 27 FEB 24 MAR 23 APR 20 MAY 18 JUNE 15 JULY 13 AUG 10 SEPT 7 OCT 5 NOV 2 NOV 30 DEC 28							SWINDON STOCK	3.10 SPOUT	27.12 P/PSR
			SWINDON set to work 4.6.12 105 882 BC 1047									SW	194 days
		25.5.12	Wheels changed L×D on Car No. 77 (0840?) Renew tyres L×D New axles (0878)										
			Stopped 11.11.12 SWINDON set to work 4.12.12										23 days
			10.12.12 SWINDON " " 14.12.12										4 "
1913	[NEWPORT] P/PGL REAR 27.12.12		JAN 25 FEB 22 MAR 22 APR 19 MAY 17 JUNE 14 JULY 12 AUG 9 SEPT 6 OCT 4 NOV 1 NOV 29 DEC 27							SWINDON TW P/PRD.	SWINDON STOCK	
			Stopped 3.3.13 SWINDON set to work 12.3.13 L 118 398 BC 1111										9 days

STEAM RAIL MOTOR CAR SHED ALLOCATIONS (SOURCE: P.R.O. RAIL 254, PIECE) CAR No 93

YEAR	DIVISION/SHED	DATE SENT FROM FACTORY											
1914	POOL ROAD	7.4.13	JAN 24	FEB 21	MAR 21	APR 18	MAY 16	JUNE 13	JULY 11	AUG 8	SEPT 5	OCT 3	OCT 31 NOV 28 DEC 26 — 79 Days
1915	STOURBRIDGE	1.12.14	JAN 23	FEB 20	MAR 20	APR 17	MAY 15	JUNE 12	JULY 10	AUG 7	SEPT 4	OCT 2	OCT 30 NOV 27 DEC 25 — 49 Days / 22
1916	STOURBRIDGE	5.11.15	JAN 22	FEB 19	MAR 18	APR 15	MAY 13	JUNE 10	JULY 8	AUG 5	SEPT 2	SEPT 30	OCT 28 NOV 25 DEC 23 — 30 Days
1917	S. WORKS		JAN 20	FEB 17	MAR 17	APR 14	MAY 12	JUNE 9	JULY 7	AUG 4	SEPT 1	SEPT 29	OCT 27 NOV 24 DEC 22 — 370 Days
1918	BRISTOL	17.8.17	JAN 19	FEB 16	MAR 16	APR 13	MAY 11	JUNE 8	JULY 6	AUG 3	AUG 31	SEPT 28	OCT 26 NOV 23 DEC 31 — 17 Days
1919	BRISTOL		JAN 18	FEB 15	MAR 15	APR 12	MAY 10	JUNE 7	JULY 5	AUG 2	AUG 30	SEPT 27	OCT 25 NOV 22 DEC 20 — 17 Days
1920			NO SHED ALLOCATIONS AVAILABLE										
1921	S. WORKS		JAN 30	FEB 27	MAR 27	APR 24	MAY 22	JUNE 19	JULY 17	AUG 14	SEPT 11	OCT 9	NOV 6 DEC 4 JAN 1 — 301 Days

STEAM RAIL MOTOR CAR SHED ALLOCATIONS (SOURCE: P.R.O. RAIL 254, PIECE)

CAR No. 93

YEAR	[DIVISION] SHED	DATE SENT FROM FACTORY														
1922	[WOLVERHMTN]	22.2.21														
	C NEWYDD		JAN 29	FEB 26	MAR 26	APR 23	MAY 21	JUNE 18	JULY 16	AUG 13	SEPT 10	OCT 8	NOV 5	DEC 3		15 Days
			✓	✓	✓	✓	✓	✓	✓	✓	✓	✓	✓	22.11B	✓	94 "
				Stopped	14.2.22	26.4.22	CROSS NEWYDD	CROSS NEWYDD	Put to work	1.3.22 R	29.7.22 R	SW			70 "
							SWINDON	"	"	"	21.11.22	H.261.681	BC.1095	DEC 31	
					12.9.22											
1923			JAN 28	FEB 25	MAR 25	APR 22	MAY 20	JUNE 17	JULY 15	AUG 12	SEPT 9	OCT 7	NOV 4	DEC 2	DEC 30	
	BRISTOL	23.11.22	✓	✓	✓	SW	✓	✓	✓	✓	✓	✓	SWINDON STOCK	7.11.6L	✓	
				Stopped	19.4.23	BRISTOL										197 Days
					7.5.23	SWINDON	Put to work	2.11.23	H.378.024	BC.1117.or9					
1924	[WORCESTER]		JAN 27	FEB 24	MAR 23	APR 20	MAY 18	JUNE 15	JULY 13	AUG 10	SEPT 7	OCT 5	NOV 2	NOV 30	DEC 28	
	GLOSTER	7.11.23	✓	✓	✓	✓	✓	✓	✓	✓	✓	✓	✓	✓	✓	
1925			JAN 25	FEB 3	MAR 22	APR 19	MAY 17	JUNE 14	JULY 12	AUG 9	SEPT 6	OCT 4	NOV 1	NOV 29	DEC 27	
	GLOSTER	7.11.23	4.1 SW	✓	3.4 GLOS	✓	OTHLF	✓	GLOS	GLOS	✓	7 CHRLF	GLOS	✓		83 Days
				Stopped	9.1.25	SWINDON	Put to work	11 AUG	2.4.25	H.319.S22	BC.1011				
1926			JAN 24	FEB 21	MAR 21	APR 18	MAY 16	JUNE 13	JULY 11	AUG 8	SEPT 5	OCT 3	OCT 31	NOV 28	DEC 26	
	GLOSTER	3.4.25	9 SW	✓	✓	✓	SWINDON STOCK	✓	19	RED 6	11 SW	✓	SWINDON STOCK		140 Days
				Stopped	8.1.26	SWINDON	Put to work	28.5.26	H.347.005	BC.1087						83 "
				"	8.10.26	SWINDON	"	"	30.12.26							
1927			JAN 23	FEB 20	MAR 20	APR 17	MAY 15	JUNE 12	JULY 10	AUG 7	SEPT 4	OCT 2	OCT 30	NOV 27	DEC 25	
	S. STOCK		23H TRAIN	✓	✓	✓	✓	NA 9 12	DH 9	✓	✓	6	12	✓	✓	
				Stopped	9.8.27	N. ABBOT	Put to work	12.8.27	H.364.658	BC.1077						3 Days
				"	12.10.27	TAUNTON	"	"	2.11.27 R							21 "
				"	11.11.27	TAUNTON	"	"	30.11.27 R							19 "
1928	[NWTN ABBOT]	12.8.27	JAN 22	FEB 19	MAR 18	APR 15	MAY 13	JUNE 10	JULY 8	AUG 5	SEPT 2	SEPT 30	OCT 28	NOV 25	DEC 23	
	TAUNTON		✓	13 22	31	✓	✓	✓	✓	4.7.H SW	✓	✓	✓	✓	✓	
				Stopped	22.2.28	TAUNTON	Put to work	21.3.28 R								27 Days
				"	21.8.28	SWINDON	H.385.649	C.1020								

STEAM RAIL MOTOR CAR SHED ALLOCATIONS (SOURCE: P.R.O. RAIL 254, PIECE

CAR No. 93

YEAR	DIVISION	SHED	DATE SENT FROM FACTORY														
1929	S WORKS			JAN 20	FEB 17	MAR 17	APR 14	MAY 12	JUNE 9	JULY 7	AUG 4	SEPT 1	SEPT 29	OCT 27	NOV 24	DEC 22	
						SWINDON YAT 8 P.M.								Out to work 20.2.29 Engine 0837 Boiler 1020		183 days

There are no further entries in "Register of Rail Motor" (P.R.O. RAIL 254 Piece 210) but are continued in further series of RAIL 254 for years when Steam Rail Motor Cars were condemned & its case of No. 93 is now for 1934 - RAIL 254 Piece 229. It is from this piece that following "red" entries are derived

1930	[BRISTOL]			JAN 18	FEB 15	MAR 15	APR 12	MAY 10	JUNE 7	JULY 5	AUG 2	AUG 30	SEPT 27	OCT 25	NOV 22	DEC 20	
	St Philips Marsh	22.2.29	YAT	✓	✓	8 P.M.											
1931	St Philips Marsh			JAN 17	FEB 14	MAR 14	APR 11	MAY 9	JUNE 6	JULY 4	AUG 1	AUG 29	SEPT 26	OCT 24	NOV 21	DEC 19	
					18 WILTON 31	SW						2H SWINDON STOCK					
				Shopped St Philips Marsh: To Swindon Fac 3/3. Put to work 27.7.31														162 days
						6	433	261	Engine 0873 Boiler 1095 (Remained with Car & end -11.34)									
1932				JAN 16	FEB 13	MAR 12	APR 9	MAY 7	JUNE 4	JULY 2	JULY 30	AUG 27	SEPT 24	OCT 22	NOV 19	DEC 17	
	S STOCK	9/31 1908	✓ 33 STOUR									6 TYPE SHOPS		1 PM STOUR			54 days
1933				Shopped 6.8.32 at Tyseley. Put to work 29.9.32								6					
				No Shed Allocations available – Record Book missing													
				Shopped 28.6.33 at Stourbridge. Put to work 20.9.33 6													84 days
				To Swindon Pool 11/7 6 Swindon Factory 11/8													
1934	[WOLVERHAMPTON]			JAN 13	FEB 10	MAR 10	APR 7	MAY 5	JUNE 3	JUNE 30	JULY 28	AUG 25	SEPT 22	OCT 20	NOV 17	DEC 15	
	STOURBRIDGE 2	8.31	✓	✓	✓ 19 MAYS S.F.P.I.											15 A 34 SW CONDEMNED	
				Shopped 20.5.34 Banbury; Swindon Pool 5/6. Condemned 17th November 1934													
				Age 26 years Total miles 479 006 with Engine 0873 and Boiler 1095													
				Completed as Trailer Car 11.5.35 LOT 1542													
				Withdrawn 19.5.56 (Down but not cut)													

signature

Main Shedding and Services Worked by Steam Rail motors across the GWR Divisions

LONDON DIVISION		
SHED	**FROM**	**TO**
Southall	Southall	Brentford
	West Drayton	Uxbridge (Vine Street)
	West Drayton	Staines
	Gerrards Cross	Uxbridge (High Street)
	Westbourne Park	Ruislip & Lekenham via Perivale & via West Ealing
	Westbourne Park	Southall (via Perivale)
	Slough	Windsor
	Park Royal	Willesden Junction
Reading	Reading	Henley-on-Thames
	Reading	Maidenhead
	Reading	Didcot
	Bourne End	Marlow
Newbury	Newbury	Lambourn
Oxford	Oxford	Princes Risborough

BRISTOL DIVISION		
SHED	**FROM**	**TO**
St Phillips Marsh	Bristol (Stapleton Road)	Clifton Road
	Bristol (Temple Meads)	Avonmouth
	Temple Meads	Portishead
Westbury & Frome	Westbury	Castle Cary
	Castle Cary	Taunton
	Westbury	Chippenham
	Westbury	Patney & Chilton
	Westbury	Warminster
	Trowbridge	Devizes
	Chippenham	Calne
Bristol & Bath	Bristol	Chippenham
Bath	Limpley Stoke	Hallatrow
Yatton	Yatton	Swindon
	Yatton	Clevedon
	Yatton	Highbridge
	Yatton	Wells
Weymouth	Weymouth	Dorchester
	Weymouth	Abbotsbury

NEWTON ABBOT DIVISION		
SHED	**FROM**	**TO**
Exeter	Exeter	Dulverton
	Exeter	Dawlish Warren
	Exeter	Heathfield
Laira & Millbay	Plymouth	Yealmpton
	Plymouth	Saltash
	Plymouth	Tavistock
St Blazey	Lostwithiel	Fowey
Taunton	Taunton	Milverton
	Taunton	Castle Cary
Truro	Truro	Newquay via Perranporth

WORCESTER DIVISION		
SHED	**FROM**	**TO**
Chalford	Chalford	Stonehouse
Cheltenham	Cheltenham	Honeybourne
Gloucester	Newham	Forest of Dean
Kidderminster	Kidderminster	Bewdley
Honeybourne	Honeybourne	Stratford-on-Avon
	Honeybourne	Evesham

NEWPORT DIVISION		
SHED	**FROM**	**TO**
Pontypool Rd	Pontypool Rd	Monmouth
	Pontypool Rd	Oakdale
Aberdare	Aberdare (low level) – Black Lion Crossing	Dare Valley Branch Cwmaman
Merthyr	Merthyr	Newport via Nine Mile Point

WOLVERHAMPTON DIVISION		
SHED	**FROM**	**TO**
Banbury	Banbury	Princes Risborough
	Banbury	Chipping Norton
Birkenhead	Rock Ferry	Ledsham
Croes Newydd	Wrexham	Rhos
	Wrexham	Coedpoeth
	Wrexham	Moss
	Wrexham	Llangollen

WOLVERHAMPTON DIVISION (cont)		
SHED	FROM	TO
Much Wenlock	Much Wenlock	Craven Arms
Stourbridge	Stourbridge Junction	Stourbridge Town
	Stourbridge J	Wolverhampton via Himley
	Dudley	Old Hill
	Langley Green	Oldbury
	Old Hill	Halesowen
Tyseley	Tyseley	Nth Warwickshire Line

NEATH DIVISION		
SHED	**FROM**	**TO**
Neath	Neath (Canal Side)	Court Sart
	Glyn Neath	Swansea East Dock
Tenby	Pembroke Dock	Tenby
Llanelli	Garnant	Gwaum-cae-Gurwen
Goodwick	Fishguard Harbour	Clarbeton Road

Main Shedding for Steam Rail Motors

Showing facilities introduced and facilities closed in the years relevant to the life of the steam rail motor system.

FACILITIES INTRODUCED OR REOPENED			FACILITIES CEASED	
STATION	**MONTH**	**YEAR**	**STATION**	**MONTH**
Chalford	Oct	**1903**	NIL	
Southall	May	**1904**	NIL	
Lambourn Valley	June			
Croes Newydd	June			
Helston (summer service only)	July			
Laira (Plymouth)	July			
Ashburton	Oct			
Evesham	Oct			
Newton Abbot	Oct			
Penzance				
Chippenham	Feb	**1905**	Ashburton	June
Corwen	July		Lambourn Valley	Aug
Exeter	July			
Frome	Oct			
Brynammon/Garnant	Mar		Ceased	May
Kidderminster				
Neath	Apr			
Newquay	Feb			
Stourbridge	Jan			

FACILITIES INTRODUCED OR REOPENED			FACILITIES CEASED	
STATION	MONTH	YEAR	STATION	MONTH
Trowbridge	Feb			
Truro	Feb			
Weymouth	Apr			
Whitland/Tenby (summer service only)	June			
Aberdare	Jan	1906	- Records not complete -	
Merthyr	Feb			
- Records missing -		1907		
Cheltenham	July	1908	NIL	
Stratford-Upon-Avon	July			
Tyseley	July			
Bristol	May	1909		
Yatton	Oct		Tenby	Oct
Radstock	July	1910	Chippenham	Oct
Didcot	May	1911		
Monmouth	July		Evesham	July
			Newquay (although intermittent use before & after)	Jan
Chester	Jan	1912	Exeter	May
Pontypool Road				
Slough	Mar	1913	Laira	Oct
Wolverhampton	May		Truro	May
Basingstoke	May	1914	NIL	
Newport	Aug	1915	Whitland	
			Aberystwyth	
			Helston	
			Tyseley	Jan
			Didcot	Mar
			Duffryn	July
			Merthyr	Mar
			Newton Abbot	Mar
			Oxford	Mar
			Radstock	Mar
Exeter	Jan	1916	Chippenham	Mar
			Neath	July
			Penzance	Mar
			Weymouth	Aug
Malvern Wells	June	1917	Goodwick	June
Neath	June		Gwaun-Cal-Gurwen	Aug
			Pontypool Road	Jan
Reading	July	1918		
Swindon	Dec		Stourbridge Junction	May
Tenby	Dec		Chalford	Nov
			Cheltenham	July
			Kidderminster	Apr/Jun
			Neath	Nov

FACILITIES INTRODUCED OR REOPENED			FACILITIES CEASED	
STATION	MONTH	YEAR	STATION	MONTH
Chippenham Truro Stourbridge	Oct July Mar	1919	Exeter Gloucester Reading Slough Worcester Swindon	Oct Mar Nov Nov May Nov
- Records missing -		1920	Tenby & Exeter	? ?
Chalford Garnant Gloucester Helston Neath Reading Weymouth Yeovil	Jul Nov Jul 1920? May 1920? Oct 1920?	1921	Weymouth	Aug
Cambrian Lines Dolgelly Lanidloes Machynlleth Oswestry Pemaen Westbury Worcester	 Sept Sept Aug Aug Dec July July	1922	Chippenham Penzance Frome	Apr Jul Dec
Birkenhead Moatlane (3 months) Neyland (3 months) Pontypool Road Weymouth	July July July July Jul–Nov	1923	Yeovil	Sept

Frome
Occasionals:
  Chester (3 months)
  Moat Lane (1 month)
  Stratford-u-Avon (1 month)
  Wolverhampton (1 month)
  Paenmenpool (5 months)
  Yatton
	Feb
	
	June
	Jul
	Jul
	Aug
	Jan
	Mar
		1924	NIL	

		1925	Oswestry Aberdare Worcester	Dec Jan Jan
NIL		1926	NIL	
Bath (reinstated)	July	1927	Bath (2 months) Bath Garnant Machynlleth Paenmanpool	M & Jun Aug Jan Aug July
NIL		1928	Chalford Frome Taunton	Feb Oct Oct
Bath Laira St Blazey Slough	Jul/Aug Jan July	1929	Gloucester Reading St Blazey Yatton	Jan Oct Aug Sep

FACILITIES INTRODUCED OR REOPENED			FACILITIES CEASED	
STATION	MONTH	YEAR	STATION	MONTH
Reading Reading Yatton Yatton	Jan Dec Jan June	**1930**	Reading Slough Yatton Yatton	Aug Aug Ap/May Aug
Yatton	Apr only	**1931**		
		1932	Pontypool Road	Sept
- Records missing -		**1933**	Birkenhead ?	
Yatton (1 month)	Apr	**1934**	Croes Newydd Exeter (spasmodic) Reading	Jan Apr Dec
NIL		**1935**	Exeter Neath St Phillip's Marsh Southall Stourbridge	June Oct Aug May Oct
ALL FACILITIES NOW ENDED AND STEAM RAIL MOTORS SOLD, SCRAPPED OR CONVERTED TO TRAILER CARS				

Great Western Area – Steam Rail Motor Routes c.1910

Alexandra (Newport) Dock and Railway

Points between which cars are run		Distance		Intermediate Stops	No. of Cars daily employed
		M	C		
Pontypridd	Caerphilly	6	40	7	2

Rymney Railway

Points between which cars are run		Distance		Intermediate Stops	No. of Cars daily employed
		M	C		
Caerphilly	Machen	4	0	3	1
Caerphilly	Senghenydd	4	40	3	

Taff Railway

Points between which cars are run		Distance		Intermediate Stops	No. of Cars daily employed
		M	C		
Aberdare (Mill St)	Pontypridd	11	43	8	2
Treherbert	Pontypridd	10	54	11	2
Maerdy	Pontypridd	9	49	8	

Points between which cars are run		Distance		Intermediate Stops	No. of Cars daily employed
		M	C		
Nelson	Pontypridd	5	70	5	1
Old Ynysybwl	Pontypridd	4	41	2	2
Aberthaw	Pontypridd	20	21	15	2 + 1 short train
Pontypridd	Cardiff	11	67	7	3 + 1 short train
Cardiff	Cadoxton	9	36	11	
Cardiff	Cardiff Docks	1	9	...	

Great Western Railway

Points between which cars are run		Distance		Intermediate Stops	No. of Cars daily employed
		M	C		
Durston	Bridgewater	5	62	2	9
Calne	Bradford S Junct	16	6	9	
Holt Junct	Patney via Devizes	13	0	3	
Weymouth	Dorchester	6	79	4	2
Upwey Junct	Abbotsbury	6	9	4	
Cheltenham	Honeybourne	21	47	10	3
Moreton	Evesham	15	9	6	
Southall	Paddington	9	6	5	5
Acton	Willesden	1	42	2	
Victoria	Gerrards Cross	22	29	17	
Ealing	Greenford	2	52	2	
Denham	Uxbridge	2	53	1	
Battersea	Clapham Junction	1	5	1	
Southall	Brentford	3	77	2	
Chester	Oswestry	26	55	11	9
Rusbon	Corwen	16	25	8	
Wrexham	Berwig	6	62	8	
Moss Valley J	Moss	1	78	4	
Rhos Junction	Wynn Hall	...	...	7	
Legacy	Ponkey	1	39	18	

Points between which cars are run		Distance		Intermediate Stops	No. of Cars daily employed
		M	C		
Worcester	Wolverhampton	33	39	19	
Hartlebury	Bridgnorth	18	6	6	
Kidderminster	Woofferton	24	10	12	9
Stourbridge J	Stourbridge Town	0	59	1	
Stourbridge J	Old Hill	4	11		
Netherton	Halesowen	4	23	6	
Birmingham	Stratford	24	74	15	
Tyseley	Henley-in-Arden	13	39	6	8
Rowington J	Bearley via Hatton	7	55	2	
Pontardulais	G C Garwen	10	66	8	
Princes Risbro'	Heyford	32	66	16	
Oxford	Shipton	18	21	4	3
Kidlington	Blenheim	3	56	…	
Port Talbot	Blaengarw	17	40	9	1
Paddington	Uxbridge	15	78	10	2
Southall	Brentford	3	31	1	
Watlington	Princes Risboro'	8	74	5	1
Banbury	Chipping Norton J	23	52	8	1
Chippenham	Calne	5	44	1	
Chippenham	Bath	12	72	4	1
Bathampton	Trowbridge	10	34	5	
Bradford S	Thingley Junction	8	29	6	
Newham	Drybrook	15	8	10	1
Weymouth	Abbotsbury	8	31	5	1
Laira	Wearde	8	11	4	
Lipson Vale	Yealmpton	7	75	6	
Laira Junct	Tavistock	13	63	8	1
Stratford	Lapworth	12	74	4	
Bearley	Hatton	5	0	1	
Pershore	Stratford	19	6	9	1
Leamington	Hatton	6	10	…	
Wrexham	Berwig	6	6	7	1
Stourbridge	Oldbury	10	30	7	1
Corwen	Rusbon	16	6	7	1
Exet St Thomas	Teignmouth	14	9	4	1

Points between which cars are run		Distance		Intermediate Stops	No. of Cars daily employed
		M	C		
Brent	St Germans	26	55	20	
Lipson Vale	Yealmpton	7	75	7	6
Tavistock J	Plymouth Bridge	1	59	2	
Truro	Penzance	25	67	10	
Black J East	Newquay	18	7	12	5
Gwinear Rd	Helston	8	67	4	
Swansea E D	British Rhondda	17	21	9	2
Aberystwyth	Lampeter	28	60	8	2
Narberth	Pembroke Dock	22	12	8	3
Tenby	Fishguard	30	22	8	2
Black Lion Cro	Cwmaman	2	56	4	2
Merthyr	Magor	33	26	12	2
Chalford	Stonehouse	6	76	8	2
Swindon	Cirencester	17	75	3	1
Chippenham	Bristol	24	31	9	
Bristol	Portishead	11	47	5	
Bristol	Chipping Sodbury	13	3	8	
Filton	Pilning	4	60	2	9
Bathampton	Taunton	52	48	19	
Westbury	Salisbury	24	44	7	
Westbury	Patney	14	38	3	

5

THE INFLUENCE OF THE STEAM RAIL MOTOR AND THE INTRODUCTION OF 'HALTS'

The growth in the number of rail motors on the GWR expanded rapidly in the early years. From the Chalford/Stonehouse run of the 12 October 1903 by 1908 the number had increased to eighty. At the February shareholders' meeting, the Chairman's speech included the following positive comment regarding the use of rail motors:

> We are proposing to extend services to find out branch lines and short sections where they will answer our purposes. I believe there is a considerable future for motor cars on rails.

That the cars would be steam had been emphasised by the Chairman to the 1903 August half-yearly meeting.

As passenger levels rose, so a need was felt for other intermediate stopping places for the convenience of passengers. Thus was established the 'Halt', a short unmanned deck or platform for local access. These were very successful (and were often installed as the result of a petition from the local community) not only in encouraging more traffic but in providing useful opposition to road transport. Thirteen were opened in 1904, followed by forty-three in 1905 and a further twenty-eight by 1907. At the beginning of the First World War in 1914, the initial thirteen had grown to 112. In addition, a number of longer platforms were sited at, for example, road crossings, some of which were manned and some not for passengers and goods from ordinary trains. So, as populations expanded, so did the availability of railway facilities. The longer platform was, as its convenience was noted, also really a must on branch lines that had proved unsuited for rail motors. Thus the longer trains had a passenger access more convenient for the train length.

These longer platforms were often manned by a senior grade who handled all the booking requirements for the passenger and goods traffic. The sportsman was also not left out of the scene of rail motor halts. The March 1907 GWR magazine carried a note which included:

> Motor halts are not only convenient for residential and marketing purposes but they afford ready means for townsfolk to reach rural districts for recreation. As illustrating this, many golf links are now served by motor halts, the following being instances:

Name of Halt	Distance from Halt to Links	Name of Club
Old Oak Lane (Acton)	¾ mile	East Acton GC
Twyford Abbey	½ mile	Hanger Hill GC
Radipole	1 mile	Weymouth Golf Links
Monkton & Came	1 mile	Weymouth Dorchester & County GC
Warren	Adjoining	Warren GC
Whitchurch (Tavistock)	¾ mile	Tavistock GC
Brimscombe Bridge	1½ miles	Minchinhampton GC
Bowbridge	½ mile	Stroud GC

The 1907 magazine also carried a note on what was to become the internal opposition to the GWR's own rail cars:

Auto Trains
These consist of a small locomotive ... 042T Type with an ordinary trailer car attached ... fitted with additional regulator gear enabling them to be driven from the footplate or the driver's compartment in the car ... electrical communication is provided from the driver's compartment on the trailer to the engine. The appearance of the combination is very pleasing, the engines having been painted brown to match the cars.

The latter painting scheme was certainly a break away from the traditional colouring of the locomotive fleet, and showed some innovative thinking on the part of the authorising person.

Also recorded in 1907 (April magazine) was a note that a halt built a couple of years before had been moved from what had been a single track to a double-track position on the new deviation line for Saltash and St Germans. The original halt had an interesting beginning. In 1905 the Royal Navy was at its peak, as was the flow of recruits to the training establishment HMS *Defiance*. A halt at the nearest available site was deemed to be a good position, with the numbers arriving, departing, going on leave etc. so, as a 'do-it-yourself' exercise, the sailors built the 'Defiance' halt themselves, with material supplied by the railway. Unlike modern-day preservation scenes, it is doubtful if the builders were volunteers although from experience it was probably a case of a CPO saying, 'I want twenty volunteers from this intake. The first twenty men in the column fall out on the left.' However, the halt was built, and when moved to its new site had been extended to platforms of 400ft length.

The early growth of railway traffic is highlighted, again in 1907, by the following note from the October 1907 issue of the GWR magazine:

> The introduction on August 3rd of a rail motor service between Newham and Bilson for passenger traffic to and from Cinderford and neighbourhood affords an excellent example of the actions that the provision of facilities develops traffic. During the first six weeks working, passengers conveyed totalled 20,324 ... There can be no doubt that but for the new service, a large proportion of these would not have undertaken a railway journey, and as the facilities could not have been provided by other than rail motors, it indicates these vehicles have met a real want.
>
> It is intended, as soon as practicable, to extend the service from Bilson to Drybrook, and arrangements are being made for cars to work out of Cinderford Joint Station by means of a loop line which is in course of construction. The present service consists of five trips each way, with one additional on Saturday evenings.

Strangely, it may be thought, the rail motor's very success contributed in no small measure to its own demise. The availability of access to such transport, the convenience of the halts and platforms on some of the more remote or difficult branch lines led to the spread of housing and population in the vicinities of the travel facility. This in its turn led to the realisation that the capacity of the rail motors was becoming too small for the growth of traffic now rapidly building up. So spread the use of small conventional locomotives (the Wolverhampton 517 tank loco is an example) and its attendant trailer cars, to which could be added milk tanks, horse boxes, goods vans and so on as occasion demanded, overshadowing completely the power and capacity of the rail motor.

Repairs or maintenance of the locomotive thus did not mean the passenger-carrying vehicles were affected, and the loco could be used by itself for shunting, something the rail motor could not do.

The power and convenience of the 'auto train' showed a convenience potential far in excess of the rail motor. From the early example of the small tank loco with a trailer car detailed in the March 1907 GWR magazine, by the end of the year 'the idea of the auto train has been enlarged upon'. A four-coach auto train had been introduced consisting of two pairs of 70ft trailers with the small locomotive between the two pairs, and was recorded as working in the Plymouth district with considerable success. The total length of this arrangement of loco and cars was 320ft, and seating was available for 312 passengers accommodated as 160 smoking and 152 non smoking seats (there were objections to smokers even then!). There were two luggage compartments and entrance to the cars was by end vestibules with a close-coupled gangway between each pair of coaches. The complete unit could be driven in the usual auto train fashion from either extremity vestibule, which was fitted with the usual connection for control of the locomotive. The regulator, giving direct control through a system of rods, levers and universal joints, electric communication, vacuum and handbrake and whistle connections were all conveniently situated for the driver. The fireman was always on the locomotive footplate (the loco in this case being a Wolverhampton 0-6-0 tank) so could 'notch up' or reverse as directed through the pre-arranged 'code' signalled by the driver. The loco was also noted as having a cab shape 'as the same cross section as the coaches' so fitted symmetrically into the group. A further locomotive, 0-6-0 tank No. 2120, was encased (1906) in a coach body section above the running plate. This proved very unpopular due to ventilation difficulties and was soon 'damaged' and removed!

By early 1908, both rail and road motor cars were in service by the Great Western. As well as the opening of a new rail motor route on 1 February for Oxford and District (see Chapter 1 for an example timetable for the new route) a recorded six-month period covering the last six months of 1907, passengers for the rail motors had been 2,816,901, while for the Company's road motors a total of 867,104 passengers had used this facility. Steam rail motor failures, listed in Chapter 3, were recorded as one in 26,900 total miles.

There was continuous expansion in the years prior to 1914–18 when the problems of war stopped or slowed many projects, and at the end of the conflict the writing on the wall pointed to a possible end of the steam rail motor. The proliferation and expansion of the rail systems, although slowed during the war, had a burst of life in the immediate aftermath. Where could additional revenue be found and how could this be achieved?

By 1923, the halt and platform question was again much to the fore, and a meeting was convened for 5 July 1923, specifically for appointed officers discussing the construction of halt platforms. It was noted that 75 per cent of their existing 234 halts were of standard height, and twelve were still of the 'low ballast' type, the latter classed as undesirable as passengers had to climb up and down from the cars by use of the footboards, which was considered a dangerous practice. The steps included in the design of the cars were recorded as 'not proving a success', and although a better version was noted in LMS use, the whole idea of steps was unsatisfactory.

A suggestion was made, and recommended, that a special type of coach with a low vestibule 1ft 6in above the ballast should be constructed, and that the steps should be internal for access from the inside of the car to the vestibule. The report of the meeting then goes on to say: 'If such a vehicle could be supplied, the halt system on branch and subsidiary lines could be extended very considerably to the advantage of the Company and travelling public.' Also noted was the requirement for additional platforms where the population exceeded 200. This burst of halt enthusiasm resulted in a further 169 halts built between 1927 and 1935.

A problem with the vestibule coach proposal was the requirement for a second access level for the conventional platform height. The low platforms were to be 150ft long with a low facing of concrete, a further idea being to eliminate the cost of wood by infilling a concrete 'box' with ballast and ash, suitably tamped and encased at the top. A standard small hut was also to be provided, say 20ft x 8ft with suitable lighting. It was also considered that at sites where trains, as well as rail motors, called the platforms should be of standard height. Reviewing the complication inherent in the low-vestibule car design, it appears that the idea was quietly shelved, no official diagram appearing in the many designs for rail motors and trailers for such a vehicle.

At the Superintendents' Meetings of 29 and 30 November 1923, a diagram (not traced in the records) was submitted for a trailer car for low-ballast platforms, and copies were circulated to the Superintendents for examination. General approval was given as the design was certainly a move toward solving the folding steps problem and the Superintendents were asked to submit any relevant comments and recommendations concerning the overall design and where they thought the cars could be used.

The procedure dragged on to the next meeting of 7 and 8 February 1924 when Minute 9974 (Halt Platforms) noted a recommendation to the General Manager for six cars to be constructed to the design already circulated, and requested suggestions for positive employment for such cars when they were officially authorised.

The meeting of 1 December 1925 (things were still dragging!) noted that construction of special cars recommended for low platforms at a cost of £2,400 per vehicle was to be held in abeyance pending an enquiry in depth into the working of branch lines generally, the subsequent report being the controlling factor. (A summary of the report is included in Chapter 8.) The report was to be compiled by the Superintendent of the line.

There was always 'the question' of 'how long should a platform be?' and the following recommendations were to be followed:

1. Light traffic to be dealt with by low ballast platforms served by the special vehicles now recommended.
2. Medium traffic platforms to be 150ft in length and of standard height.
3. Heavy traffic; length of platforms to be governed by the length of the trains or cars calling, as 'pulling up' should be avoided.

On branches where there are a number of halts, the platforms should ... be of uniform length to avoid having to load passengers in selected vehicles, making it necessary for drivers to stop at particular spots.

A rethink was required for number one above, in the light of requirements and fate of the 'special vehicles' mentioned.

It was noted that the Ministry of Transport requirements did not make specific reference to halts or platforms. Trains of varying lengths were already calling at 127 places regarded as halts or platforms, and, other than the waiting sheds previously mentioned, twenty-eight places had additional accommodation, eighteen had lavatory facilities and at thirty-four sites no shelter at all was provided on the platform.

Ministry of Transport requirements for stations, as opposed to halts or platforms (the latter introduced after the stations legislation was implemented) included provision of lavatory accommodation, shelters and clocks, and the standard height of platforms.

To ensure easier access to the halts and platforms, the company often introduced a footpath or a flight of steps from a bridge to reduce the distances from the country road to suitable access points. There were also at this time proposals for handling milk and parcels where convenient, as handling these commodities already existed at fifty-four places coming under the halt or platform category. It was noted that at the Wales section, milk churns were handled from ballast level by means of a specially designed slide, and it was considered desirable to expand use of this slide wherever possible. Such ease of handling had a potential for creating or developing such traffic and should not be overlooked. It was further emphasised that selected sites should preferably contain potential for expansion into stations with siding capacity. Although desirable, the very nature of many branch line environs precluded such an idea.

The steam rail motor was also integrated into main-line running, as interwoven and intermediate services were introduced to ensure that, if possible, all passengers had access to the mainline routes from the smaller places where the mainline expresses did not stop. A further facility was the use of the 'slip coach' from certain express runs. The coach would be automatically released, or 'slipped' from a speeding train and, carefully controlled, running freely into its allocated station, its express train now long gone. As examples of this, an express journey from, say, Paddington to Bath would include a slip coach to be released at Chippenham. The coach would then be picked up by a steam rail motor and would call at all intermediate stations between its slip point and final destination at Bath. The only disadvantage, following a rapid transit from Paddington to its point of slip, was that passengers had no access to dining cars and so on, being isolated in the slip coach on the tail of the express.

From the introduction of the steam rail motor in 1903, and overlapping the demise of the rail motor into the era of the auto train and its separate locomotive of conventional design, a total of about 420 halts and platforms were introduced along with about three dozen on the absorption of the Welsh railways on the amalgamation, when the 'Big Four' were born.

The GWR halts and platforms programme proved the inspiration for other railways to follow suit, as soon as their convenience and potential for additional passenger traffic was recognised. The GWR was, however, to remain way ahead of the others, opening twice as many halts and platforms as all the other railways put together.

On the eventual demise of the steam rail motors of the GWR, a lasting legacy was added traffic generated from introduction of the halts, all down to the steam rail motor and its trailer cars.

6

THE BRANCHES OF THE GWR AND THE RAIL MOTOR

The original concept of the GWR had been to join the capital, London, with the western cities of Bristol and Bath, almost at the time ignoring the areas in between. At the time of the railway boom years, many companies were formed and short lines built as well as the 'cross country' routes covering the areas between towns and villages where a railway transport system was thought to have a profitable future, and linking with, or in the vicinity of, the main rail routes.

Thus were introduced a number of shortish lines, which, constructed by small companies later absorbed into the GW system, had followed tight economic limitations. The resulting lines thus had curves and gradients built that followed the easiest and flattest contours of the ground. In the later broad picture of the growing total system, such limitations would have been unacceptable due to radius and steepness problems. All these were to combine to add to the running costs of branch trains due to weight limits and speed restrictions but were 'fait accompli' on the absorption of the tracks.

In later years, certain of the branches, as the short lines inevitably became, were built under the Authority of Orders obtained under the Light Railways Act of 1896, and were:

1. Wrington Vale (Congresbury and Blagdon) (1897)
2. Cleobury Mortimer and Ditton Priors (1901)
3. Lampeter and Aberayon (1906)
4. Vale of Rheidol (Aberystwyth and Devils Bridge (1897–1902)
5. Welshpool and Llanfair (1899–1905)
6. Dinas Mawd (1910)
7. Tanat Valley (Llynelys and Llangynog) (1898–1901)

Others already absorbed were built under Light Railway Orders obtained before the 1896 Act.

In branch line terminology, there were those referred to as 'subsidiary branch lines' to differentiate them from what became really extensions of the mainline (for example Windsor and Kingwear). A further division was made of the subsidiary lines into two classifications:

1. Branches which are self-contained and are worked by services that entail a change for passengers at the junction station. The 'through' traffic being for goods only.
2. Branches served eventually by trains, auto services or rail motors between the branch and local businesses, shopping or market centre on the mainline.

In terms of the cost based on the three types of motive power for the trains, to include running, maintenance and renewal costs, returns showed that the rail motors were the cheapest option, giving some confirmation to the reasons for adoption, but there were recognised problems. On some branch lines, the employment of a steam engine (as opposed to auto engines and rail motors) was a requirement conditioned by the need to move heavier traffic (e.g. coal and timber) than could be coped with by the other means available. This also entailed the uneconomic use of the engines to run the limited passenger traffic. The auto engines were a better bet in certain circumstances, as being cheaper to run, additional trailer cars could be added, from the end of which the locomotive could be controlled, thus eliminating running around the train for a return journey.

The goods or freight traffic on the routes may be split into three groups:

1. General merchandise and perishables – prompt delivery and transport being essential. Later such goods would be carried by an emerging opposition: road transport.
2. Heavy traffic – this comprised often routing and regular movements of grain, timber, coal and road stone, and was the predominant requirement on almost all branches, although rapid 'perishable' transport was not needed.
3. Private siding traffic – a limited amount of private siding traffic, which could vary from perishable items to manufactured goods.

Because of the nature of the general traffic on a number of branch routes, the problems of diversity were solved to some extent by a 'mixed traffic' formula, whereby passengers and freight were conveyed in one train. There were problems inherent in this system, occasioning delays to passengers caused by the necessary shunting of some wagons on various stops along the line. Of the total number of branch lines, nine had no separate goods traffic at all, all goods being transported under the 'mixed' formula in which the nominally non-urgent or slower moving goods had the benefit of a regular passenger service. Because of the closed communities on many of the branch lines, the flow of traffic, both passenger and goods, could be predicted, not with any accuracy it must be admitted but accurately enough for timetables to be set out to cover fairs, market days and so on and possibly heavier traffic at particular times. Such quietly moving rural scenes were soon to be changed forever following 1914–18.

Whilst the steam rail motor came to prominent use at the beginning of the century, the section showing diagrams of 70ft-long motors should not be allowed to confuse the reader into the impression that such vehicles could be used ad hoc on all branches. Most coaches in this application were of the small six- and even four-wheel design. These formed various lengths of trains of up to five coaches, governed by the sharp curves built into the systems when originally set out.

On these subsidiary branches, which consisted of single lines (there were only two exceptions), the signalling was to one of the three train staff systems of the Ministry of Transport:

1. Electric Staff, Tablet or Token with loops for crossing trains on the busier and longer branches. Thirty-two of the fifty-three listed branches work to this system. Instrumentation, costly to provide and maintain was required for this type of operation. The associated very detailed regulations involved suitably skilled and experienced personnel to operate safely.
2. Block Telegraph and Train Staff and Ticket. Three of the fifty-three listed branches used this method, which was cheaper to administer.
3. With only one engine in steam on the branch, the Wooden Staff system was the least expensive, requiring a minimum of signalling and no highly skilled staff and much lower maintenance costs.

Notes related to the systems defined above:

1.	To make full use of the most heavily used lines, a closely monitored and controlled system was essential, particularly for crossing trains, where, as in all cases, safety was paramount.
2 & 3	With the 'one engine in steam' system, all of the related 'points' were locked out with a key on the train staff. As the staff itself must be carried on the engine, no points could be moved without the sole engine being present. The only signals required on these branches were at the junction, with a fixed distant signal permanently set at 'danger' at the branch terminal station, really as a marker for bad-visibility conditions. Public level crossings were also covered by distant signals. Thus no block telegraph instruments were required.
4.	Dependent upon the position of the branch junction with the main line, certain circumstances, for example where the junction station was some distance from main connection, determined the siting and manning of a signal box, the box really divorced from main-line working.

A further branch-line problem, indirectly associated with signalling, was the staffing of the numerous level crossings to control gates and access. The crossings had been installed by the builders of the branches to avoid the costs into the 1930s.

Track maintenance on any single line is always a problem when 'occupation' is required, and to allow this, probably much against the grain, the road transport was used for the daily routine of passenger traffic during the working day. This was introduced as the growing competition with road vehicles developed as the latter traffic expanded over the years. For the periods of occupation, the goods traffic was scheduled for early and late shifts before and after the usual 'nine to five' working day.

On the subject of road transport, there came a situation, again as road transport developed, that, not confined to branch lines, the rail system came into competition with its own road transport. With the general growth of the rural scene – new houses, roads and so on – the branch lines became the means of transporting the road stone and fuel oils used by its main competitors, thus working, it was thought, towards its own demise. (In effect history was repeating itself after the canals had carried the materials for the railway builders.)

Various branch-line requirements of the early years tend to be overlooked in retrospect, but station lighting on the branches during the life of the steam rail motor and its steam-associated motive power was by oil lamp, a great innovation, recorded with the introduction during the 1920s of the 'Tilley' oil lamp, a big improvement on the previously used wick-type lamps. A further requirement of steam is water and the tanks at various watering points were filled by steam pumps connected as required to the steam supply of the branch locomotive, it being cheaper than purchasing water from the local authority when you owned your own well!

While the end of the steam rail motor was in sight by the 1920s, the introduction of new branch lines was still occurring. The Earl of Dudley, quite an extensive landowner, opened several new collieries in the area of Baggeridge, near Himley, and to serve this new industrial area the Kingswinford branch was opened in May 1925. This ran from Brettell Lane to Oxley, for which the existing first three miles of the Kingswinford Mineral Line was relayed and doubled, leaving the rest to Oxley as single track. The employment of the steam rail motors suited what turned out to be a dwindling number of passengers, thus the passenger service was withdrawn in 1932, goods traffic continuing until 1965 and the line itself used as an avoiding route for Snow Hill–Wolverhampton traffic. So, while branch lines, low platform halts, and low ballast pickups continued, the amount of traffic generated was too much for the steam rail motor concept, which was concluded in 1935.

Branch Operating Details – 1925

Branch	No.	A) Passenger Traffic worked by: B) Goods Traffic worked by:	Engine Stabled
ABBOTSBURY	1	A) Rail motors working to & from Weymouth B) Goods train	Weymouth
ABERAYRON & LAMPETER	2	A) Auto train B) 1 train each way	Aberayron
ABEMULE & KERRY	3	A) Branch train B) Goods train RR	Kerry
ABINGDON	4	A) Branch train B) 2 trains each way – mixed	Abingdon
ALCASTER	5	A) Auto train B) 2 trains each way – mixed	Alcaster
ASHBURTON	6	A) Branch train B) 1 train each way	Ashburton
BLENHEIM	7	A) Branch train B) 1 each way – mixed	Blenheim
BRENTFORD	8	A) Auto trains B) -	Southall
BRIDPORT	9	A) Branch train B) 1 down mixed train 2 up – 1 mixed	Bridport
BRIXHAM	10	A) Branch train B) 1 train each way – mixed	Brixham
CALNE	11	A) Auto train & rail motors B) 3 trips each way	Chippenham
CHARD	12	A) Branch trains B) Goods train – 2 trips each way	Taunton
CIRENCESTER	13	A) Branch train B) 1 Goods train each way	Cirencester
CLEVEDON	14	A) Branch train / Rail motor B) 1 Goods train each way	Yatton
CLEOBURY MORTIMER & DITTON PRIORS	15	A) Branch trains B) 1 Goods train each way	Cleobury Town
CLYNDERWEN & LETTERSTON	16	A) Branch train B) 1 Goods train	Fishguard
DINAS MAWDDWY	17	A) Branch train B) Mixed trains	Dinas Mawddwy
CROXLEY	18	A) Branch train B) Mixed train	Kington

Trips	Signalling Arrangements
5 trips each way 2 Sat only; Mon, Wed, Fri only	WOODEN STAFF One engine in steam
4 trips each way	ELECTRIC TRAIN STAFF Crossing place at Felin Fach
3 'mixed' trains each way	WOODEN STAFF One engine in steam
14 trips & 3 mixed trips 15 trips & 2 mixed trips	TRAIN STAFF & TICKET
6 trips each way	ELECTRIC TABLET No crossing place
7 trips each way	TRAIN STAFF AND TICKET WORKING
Down: 9 incl 1 mixed & 1 thro' train Up: 9 trips incl 3 mixed & 1 thro' train	ELECTRIC TRAIN STAFF
25 trips each way	DOUBLE LINE BLOCK TELEGRAPH WORKING between Southall East Station and Brentford
4 trips Maiden Newton to West Bay return (1 mixed) 3 trips MN to Bridport return	ELECTRIC STAFF Crossing place at Bridport
16 trips each way (1 mixed) 21 mixed RR – 1 trip return Wed & Sat only	ELECTRIC TRAIN TOKEN
8 trips each way 1 trip Sat only	ELECTRIC TRAIN STAFF No crossing place
6 trips 1 Sat only	ELECTRIC TRAIN STAFF & TABLET No crossing. Staff at watch & Ilminster. Special switching apparatus at Hatch
Down: 11 trips (12 Mon) (1 mixed) Up: 10 trips (11 Mon) (4 mixed)	ELECTRIC TRAIN STAFF
3 trips into Clevedon – 3 trips out Clevedon 18 trips each way / 1 trip each way Wed, Sat into Clevedon / out Clevedon (mixed)	WOODEN STAFF One engine in steam. **Note:** Branch rail motors work from Yatton to Clevedon without guard.
3 trips each way (2 mixed down) 1 mixed up / mixed on Wednesdays	WOODEN STAFF One engine in steam
3 mixed to Clynderwen to Fishguard & Goodwick 2 mixed on return mixed & 1 Goods	WOODEN STAFF 1 engine in steam Clynderwen to Letterston ELECTRIC STAFF Letterston to Letterston Junction (crossing loops at Lett.. & Maenclochog)
5 trips each way (mixed)	WOODEN STAFF One engine in steam
3 trips Kington to Eardisley Return 3 mixed of 6	WOODEN STAFF One engine in steam

Branch	No.	A) Passenger Traffic worked by: B) Goods Traffic worked by:	Engine Stabled
EXE VALLEY	19	A) Auto train B) 1 Goods train	Exeter
FALMOUTH	20	A) Branch train B) 2 Goods trains	Truro
FARINGDON	21	A) 11 trains B) 9 trains	Faringdon
HEMYOCK	22	A) Branch train B) (Mixed trains)	Hemyock
HIGHWORTH	23	A) Branch train / Branch train B) 1 train / 1 train	Swindon
LAMBOURN	24	A) Trains incl trailer for use at halts B) 1 train	Lambourn
LAUNCESTON	25	A) Branch trains B) 3 Goods trains / 1 Goods train	Launceston & Laira
LLANTRISANT & ABERTHAW	26	A) 9 Branch trains / 2 Branch trains B) 1 train / 1 train	Llantrisant
LLANYMYNECK & LLANFYLLIN	27	A) Trains and 1 Auto train B) 1 train	Llanfyllin
LEOMINSTER & NEW RADNOR	28	A) Branch trains B) 1 train	Kington & Leominster
LISKEARD & LOOE	29	A) Trains B) Train	Moorswater
MALMESBURY	30	A) Branch trains B) Branch train	Malmesbury
MINEHEAD	31	A) Trains (extra train in summer) B) Train	Minehead & Taunton
MORETON-HAMPSTEAD	32	A) Train 1 Rail motor B) Train	Moreton-Hampstead

Trips	Signalling Arrangements
7 trips Exeter to Dulverton – 1 trip Thurs & Sat only – Exeter to Dulverton return	ELECTRIC TRAIN STAFF Crossing places at Thorverton, Cadeleigh, Tiverton & Bampton
15 trips each way (1 down trip mixed) Each way. 1 mixed	ELECTRIC TRAIN STAFF Crossing places at Perranwel & Penryn
11 trips each way Down: 5 mixed Up: 4 mixed 5 mixed into Faringdon – 4 mixed out of Faringdon	TRAIN STAFF AND TICKET
5 trips each way 4 of them mixed Mixed as above	WOODEN STAFF One engine in steam
6 trips each way (1 mixed) / 1 trip each way MSO Each way / Each way RR	WOODEN STAFF One engine in steam
5 trips each way Each way	ELECTRIC TABLET Crossing place at Welford Park
4 thro' to Launceston; 11 to Tavistock; 1 Sat only (down & up) 3 trips each way / 1 trip thro' to Launceston	ELECTRIC STAFF All stations are crossing stations except Coryton and Mary Tavy
Llantrisant to Cowbridge / Llantrisant to Aberthaw. All trips return 1 trip Llantrisant to Aberthaw return 3 trips Llantrisant to Llanharry return	ELECTRIC STAFF Crossing at Cowbridge Junction **Note:** Special occupation key to permit trains to work from C when A is closed.
5 trips each way; 1 trip each way Sat only; 1 trip each way Wed only 1 trip each way and 1 Wed only trip each way	ELECTRIC STAFF Crossing place at Llansantffraid **Note:** Proposal to convert to light railway.
3 trips Kington/Leominster; 3 trips Leominster to New Radnor. All return 1 trip return	ELECTRIC TRAIN STAFF Kington J to Kington – crossing places at Titley & Pembridge ELECTRICAL TRAIN KEY Kington as a crossing station; 1 engine in steam
Down: 7 trips (1 Mixed) / Up: 8 trips 1 trip each way	ELECTRIC TABLET Crossing place at Coombe Junction WOODEN STAFF Coombe Junction to Moorswater
7 trips each way 3 trips inwards mixed / 3 outwards mixed	WOODEN STAFF One engine in steam **Note:** It was proposed to try a Sentinel rail motor on this branch
7 trips each way 1 trip complete branch each way / 1 trip Taunton to Washford return	ELECTRIC TRAIN STAFF Crossing stations at Bishops Lydeard, Crowcombe, Williton & Blue Anchor **Note:** Dunster & Watchet to be discontinued as train staff stations and boxes closed.
10 trips each way 1 trip each way 13 trips each way thro'out branch 2 trips Newton Abbot to Heathfield return	ELECTRIC TRAIN STAFF & TABLET Crossing station Bovey

Branch	No	A) Passenger Traffic worked by: B) Goods Traffic worked by:	Engine Stabled
MOSS VALLEY	33	A) Rail motor B) Rail motor	Wrexham
NEWCASTLE EMLYN	34	A) Branch trains B) Goods trains	Newcastle Emlyn
PEMBROKE & WHITLAND	35	A) Auto Cars & Branch trains B) Goods	Tenby & Whitland
PONTRILAS & HAY	36	A) Trains (mixed) B) Trains (mixed)	Pontrilas
PRESTEIGN	37	A) Branch train B) Branch train	Kington
PRINCETOWN	38	A) Branch train B) Branch train	Princetown
ST IVES	39	A) Branch train B) Branch train	St Ives
SHIPSTON-ON-STOUR	40	A) Train B) Train	Worcester
TANAT VALLEY LINE	41	A) Branch train B) Branch train	Oswestry
TEIGN VALLEY	42	A) Auto train and Rail motor B) Auto train	Exeter
TETBURY	43	A) Branch train B) Branch train	Tetbury
VALE OF RHEIDOL	44	A) Branch train of specially constructed coaches B) Branch train	Aberystwyth (Narrow gauge 1' 11½")
WADEBRIDGE	45	A) Branch trains (proposal for auto trains) B) Trains	Bodmin
WALLINGFORD	46	A) Branch train B) Branch train	Wallingford
WELLINGTON	47	A) Branch train (incl trailer for use at halts) B) Branch train	Watlington

Trips	Signalling Arrangements
9 trips each way; 3 Sat only trips 4 trips each way	ELECTRIC TRAIN STAFF Between Moss Valley J & Moss Crossing WOODEN STAFF Moss Crossing to Bryn Mally Colliery **Note:** Discontinuance of Rail motor; replace Electric Staff by Wooden Staff
6 trips each way; 1 trip each way not Sat 2 trips each way with extra RR trips	ELECTRIC TRAIN STAFF WORKING Crossing places at Llandyssul & Henllan
Up: 4 thro'out branch Down: 5 thro'out branch Up: 2 auto trips thro'out branch Down: 5 short trips (Mon, Fri, Sat) 2 trips tho'out branch each way 2 short trips	ELECTRIC TRAIN STAFF Crossing stations at Narberth, Templeton, Tenby, Saundersfoot, Manorbier, Pembroke
3 trips each way (1 Pontrilas/Dorstone return) 1 trip each way Thurs only 1 trip Pontrilas to Dorstone return Wed only	WOODEN STAFF One engine in steam **Note:** Proposal for all passenger traffic by road motor service.
3 trips Kington to Presteign return; 1 trip Wed only; 1 mixed trip each way; 2 RR goods each direction 1 runs one day per week 1 runs one day per 2 weeks	WOODEN STAFF One engine in steam
5 trips each way; 1 trip Sat & Wed only; all mixed Goods run 3 days/week	ELECTRIC TRAIN STAFF Station at Dousland
15 trips each way 1 goods each way	ELECTIC TRAIN STAFF No crossing place
3 trips mixed each way 3 trips mixed each way	WOODEN STAFF One engine in steam. No block telegraph
1 trip daily; 1 Wed & Sat only; 2 Wed & Sat excepted; 2 Wed only; 1 Sat only 1 trip each way; additional on certain days	ELECTRIC TABLET Crossing places at Porthywaen, Blodwell Junctn, Llangeow & Llanrhaiadr Mochnant
6 trips each way; 1 Sat only; 1 Wed, Fri & Sat only 3 trips each way (1 to Christow only)	ELECTRIC TRAIN STAFF Crossing places Christow & Trusham (by shunting)
6 trips each way (2 mixed) 1 trip each way (2 mixed trains)	ELECTRIC TRAIN STAFF No crossing station
Winter: 3 trips each way (2 mixed) 1 mixed each way Mon & Sat or Summer: 7 each way; 5 each way Sat only All mixed	WINTER WOODEN STAFF One engine in steam SUMMER ELECTRIC TRAIN STAFF Crossing stations Aberffrwd & Chapel Bangor
10 trips each way; 13 Bodmin Rd to Bodmin 3 trips each way with 7 RR trips. Heavy traffic ex Southern Line	ELECTRIC TRAIN STAFF Bodmin Rd to Bodmin & Bodmin to Boscarne Junction
13 trips ex Wallingford; 14 trips ex Cholsey; 1 Sat only 1 Goods train ex Cholsey	WOODEN STAFF One engine in steam
5 trips each way & 1 trip Saturdays 2 trips each way; 1 Princes Risborough to Chinnor & return	WOODEN STAFF One engine in steam

Branch	No	A) Passenger Traffic worked by: B) Goods Traffic worked by:	Engine Stabled
WELSHPOOL & LLANFAIR	48	A) Branch train B) Branch train	Welshpool (narrow gauge 2'6")
WREXHAM BRYMBO & MINERA	49	A) Steam Rail motor B) Trains	Wrexham
WREXHAM & RHOS	50	A) Steam Rail motor B) Branch train	Wrexham
WHITLAND & CARDIGAN	51	A) Branch trains B) Branch trains	Cardigan
WRINGTON VALE	52	A) Branch train; Steam Rail motor B) Branch train	Yatton (light railway)
YEALMPTON	53	A) Auto train B) Auto train	Plymouth

It will be noted from this detail that the influence and use of the rail motor had, by 1925, almost vanished. Those still in use were under close scrutiny with the threat of withdrawal ever present.

Trips	Signalling Arrangements
3 trips each way daily mixed; 1 mixed 3 times per week All mixed	**WOODEN STAFF** One engine
4 trips to Berwig return 6 trips to Coed Poeth return 4 trips to Brymbo return 3 Saturdays only trips All Goods trains	**DOUBLE LINE BLOCK TELEGRAPH** Croes Newydd & Brymbo West crossing **ELECTRIC TRAIN STAFF** Between Brymbo West crossing & Berwig siding. Crossing place at Coed Poeth **WOODEN STAFF** Berwig siding & Minera. One engine in steam **Note:** Reduction in rail motor services and discontinuance between Coed Poeth and Berwig recommended
13 trips each way 4 Saturday only trips 1 trip each way	**ELECTRIC TRAIN STAFF** Rhos Junction to Brook Street. Crossing places at Rhos Jnctn, Legacy (one platform only) and Rhos
4 trips each way (3 mixed trains) 2 trips each way (1 cattle train monthly)	**ELECTRIC STAFF** Crossing places at Llanglydwen, Crymmech Arms & Boncath
3 trips return; 1 trip return 1 Goods train each way	**WOODEN STAFF** One engine in steam
9 trips each way; 1 trip Wed, Thurs & Sat only 1 trip each way	**ELECTRIC STAFF** Between Plymstock & Yealpton. No crossing place

7

THE DIFFICULTIES OF THE BRANCH LINES

A problem soon acknowledged with the steam rail motors was associated with the gradients faced when running on branch lines in rural areas. The following are examples of some of the many gradient diagrams that covered the whole GWR system, being a selection indicative of the 'ups and downs' faced by the steam motors that did not have the power of a small 0-6-0 or 0-4-2 locomotive, and thus found difficulty with added loads of goods wagons, cattle trucks and so on.

These difficulties were to be highlighted in a 1925 report on branch-line operation, detailed summaries of which are included in Chapter 8.

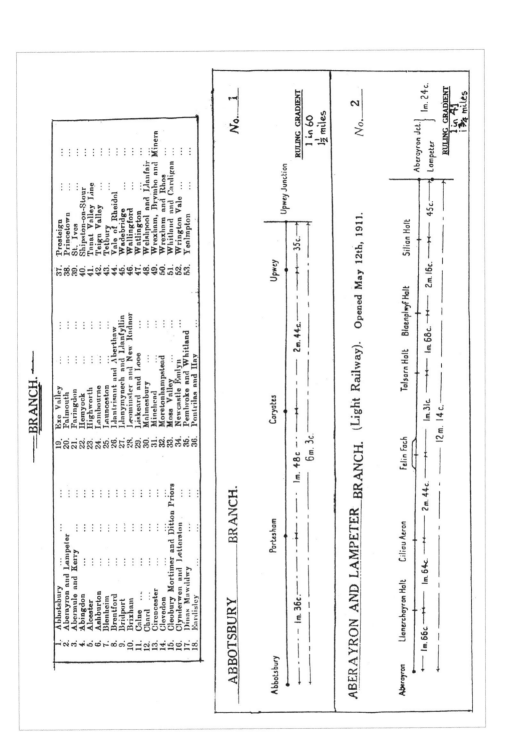

BRANCH.

1. Abbotsbury
2. Aberayron and Lampeter
3. Abermule and Kerry
4. Abingdon
5. Alcester
6. Ashburton
7. Blenheim
8. Brentford
9. Bridport
10. Brixham
11. Calne
12. Chard
13. Cirencester
14. Clevedon
15. Cleobury Mortimer and Ditton Priors
16. Clynderwen and Letterston
17. Dinas Mawddwy
18. Fairlisley

19. Exe Valley
20. Falmouth
21. Faringdon
22. Hemyock
23. Highworth
24. Lambourne
25. Launceston
26. Llantrisant and Aberthaw
27. Llanymynech and Llanfyllin
28. Leominster and New Radnor
29. Liskeard and Looe
30. Malmesbury
31. Minehead
32. Moretonhampstead
33. Moss Valley
34. Newcastle Emlyn
35. Pembroke and Whitland
36. Pontrilas and Hay

37. Presteign
38. Princetown
39. St. Ives
40. Shipston-on-Stour
41. Tanat Valley Line
42. Teign Valley
43. Tetbury
44. Vale of Rheidol
45. Wadebridge
46. Wallingford
47. Watlington
48. Welshpool and Llanfair
49. Wrexham, Brymbo and Minera
50. Wrexham and Rhos
51. Whitland and Cardigan
52. Wrington Vale
53. Yealmpton

ABBOTSBURY BRANCH.

Abbotsbury — 1m. 36c. — Portesham — 1m. 48c. — Coryates — 2m. 44c. — Upwey — 35c. — Upwey Junction

6m. 3c.

No. 1

RULING GRADIENT
1 in 60
1½ miles

ABERAYRON AND LAMPETER BRANCH. (Light Railway). Opened May 12th, 1911.

Aberayron — 1m. 66c. — Llanerchayron Holt — 1m. 64c. — Ciliau Aeron — 2m. 44c. — Felin Fach — 1m. 31c. — Talsarn Holt — 1m. 68c. — Blaenplwyf Holt — 2m. 16c. — Silian Holt — 45c. — Aberayron Jct. } 1m. 24c. — Lampeter

12m. 14c.

No. 2

RULING GRADIENT
1 in 4¼
1¾ miles

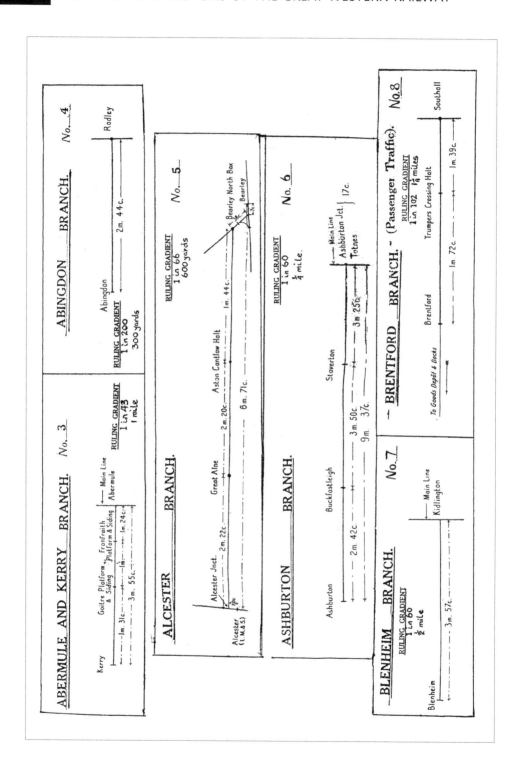

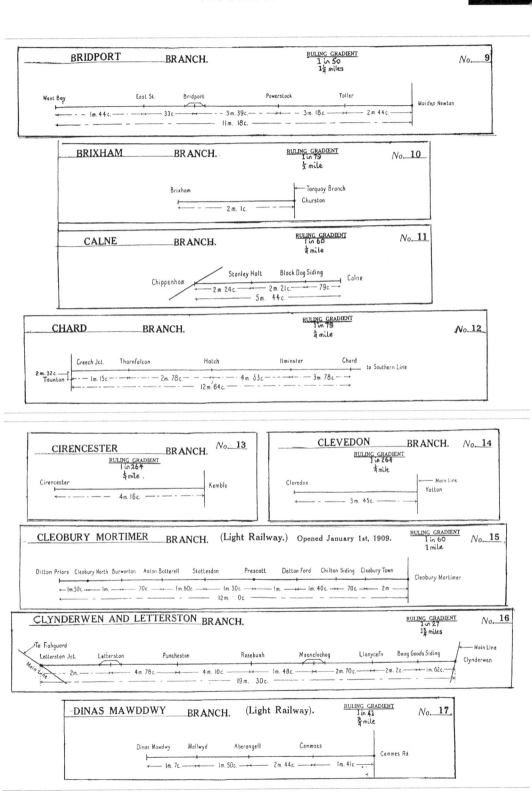

BRIDPORT ————— BRANCH.

RULING GRADIENT
1 in 50
1½ miles

No. 9

West Bay East St. Bridport Powerstock Toller Maiden Newton
— — 1m. 44c. — — — · — 33c. — · — — 3m. 39c. — — · — — 3m. 18c. — · — — 2m. 44c. — ·
— — — — — — — — — — 11m. 18c. — — — — — — — —

BRIXHAM ————— BRANCH.

RULING GRADIENT
1 in 79
½ mile

No. 10

Brixham Torquay Branch
Churston
— — — — 2m. 1c. — — — — ·

CALNE ————— BRANCH.

RULING GRADIENT
1 in 60
¾ mile

No. 11

Chippenham Stanley Halt Black Dog Siding Calne
— 2m. 24c. — · — 2m. 21c. — · — 79c. — ·
— — — — 5m. 44c. — — — —

CHARD ————— BRANCH.

RULING GRADIENT
1 in 79
¼ mile

No. 12

2m. 32c. Creech Jct. Thornfalcon Hatch Ilminster Chard to Southern Line
Taunton — 1m. 15c. — · — 2m. 78c. — — · — 4m. 53c. — — · — 3m. 78c. — ·
— — — — — — 12m. 64c. — — — — — —

CIRENCESTER ————— BRANCH. No. 13

RULING GRADIENT
1 in 264
¼ mile

Cirencester Kemble
— — — — 4m. 16c. — — — — ·

CLEVEDON ————— BRANCH. No. 14

RULING GRADIENT
1 in 264
¼ mile

Clevedon Main Line
Yatton
— — 3m. 45c. — — ·

CLEOBURY MORTIMER ————— BRANCH. (Light Railway.) Opened January 1st, 1909.

RULING GRADIENT
1 in 60
1 mile

No. 15

Ditton Priors Cleobury North Burwarton Aston Botterell Stottesdon Prescott Detton Ford Chilton Siding Cleobury Town Cleobury Mortimer
— 1m. 50c. — · — 1m. — · — 70c. — · — 1m. 60c. — · — 1m. 30c. — · — 1m. — · — 1m. 40c. — · — 70c. — · — 2m. —
— — — — — — — 12m. 0c. — — — — — — —

CLYNDERWEN AND LETTERSTON ————— BRANCH.

RULING GRADIENT
1 in 27
1⅛ miles

No. 16

To Fishguard Main Line
Letterston Jct. Letterston Puncheston Rosebush Maenclochog Llanycefn Boag Goods Siding Clynderwen
Main Line — 2m. — · — 4m. 78c. — · — 4m. 10c. — · — 1m. 48c. — · — 2m. 70c. — · — 2m. 2c. — · — 1m. 62c. —
— — — — — — 19m. 30c. — — — — — —

DINAS MAWDDWY ————— BRANCH. (Light Railway).

RULING GRADIENT
1 in 41
¾ mile

No. 17

Dinas Mawddwy Mallwyd Abrangell Cemmaes Cemmes Rd.
— 1m. 7c. — · — 1m. 50c. — · — 2m. 44c. — · — 1m. 41c. —

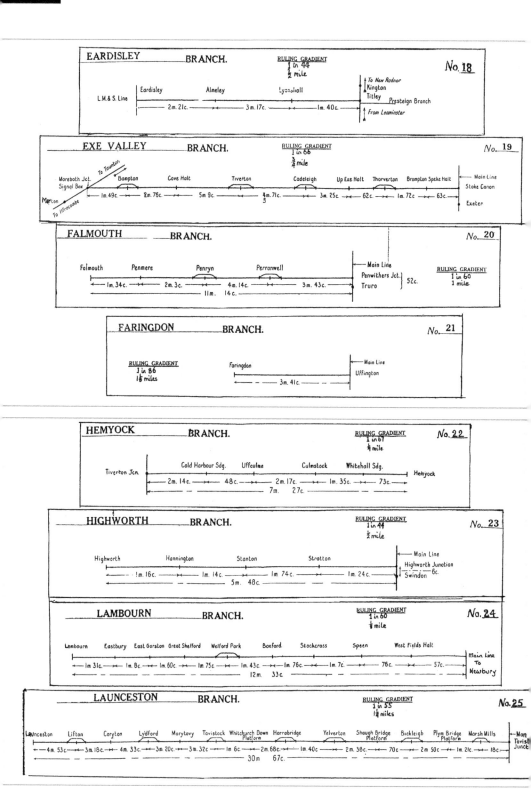

EARDISLEY — BRANCH.

RULING GRADIENT
1 in 44
½ mile

No. 18

L.M.& S. Line | Eardisley | Almeley | Lyonshall | To New Radnor / Kington / Titley / Presteign Branch / From Leominster

— 2m. 21c. — 3m. 17c. — 1m. 40c. —

EXE VALLEY — BRANCH.

RULING GRADIENT
1 in 66
¾ mile

No. 19

Moreboth Jct. Signal Box / Morton / To Taunton / To Ilfracombe | Bampton | Cove Halt | Tiverton | Cadeleigh | Up Exe Halt | Thorverton | Brampton Speke Halt | Main Line / Stoke Canon / Exeter

— 1m. 49c. — 2m. 76c. — 5m 9c. — ⅗m. 71c. — 3m. 25c. — 62c. — 1m. 72c. — 63c. —

FALMOUTH — BRANCH.

No. 20

Falmouth | Penmere | Penryn | Perranwell | Main Line / Penwithers Jct. / Truro
— 1m. 34c. — 2m. 3c. — 4m. 14c. — 3m. 43c. — 52c.
— 11m. 14c. —

RULING GRADIENT
1 in 60
1 mile

FARINGDON — BRANCH.

No. 21

RULING GRADIENT
1 in 88
1⅜ miles

Faringdon | Main Line / Uffington
— 3m. 41c. —

HEMYOCK — BRANCH.

RULING GRADIENT
1 in 61
¾ mile

No. 22

Tiverton Jcn. | Cold Harbour Sdg. | Uffculme | Culmstock | Whitehall Sdg. | Hemyock
— 2m. 14c. — 48c. — 2m. 17c. — 1m. 35c. — 73c. —
— 7m. 27c. —

HIGHWORTH — BRANCH.

RULING GRADIENT
1 in 44
½ mile

No. 23

Highworth | Hannington | Stanton | Stratton | Main Line / Highworth Junction / Swindon 6c.
— 1m. 16c. — 1m. 14c. — 1m 74c. — 1m. 24c. —
— 5m. 48c. —

LAMBOURN — BRANCH.

RULING GRADIENT
1 in 60
⅞ mile

No. 24

Lambourn | Eastbury | East Garston | Great Shefford | Welford Park | Boxford. | Stockcross | Speen | West Fields Halt | Main Line / To / Newbury
— 1m 31c. — 1m. 8c. — 1m. 60c. — 1m 75c. — 1m. 43c. — 1m 76c. — 1m. 7c. — 76c. — 57c. —
— 12m. 33c. —

LAUNCESTON — BRANCH.

RULING GRADIENT
1 in 55
1¼ miles

No. 25

Launceston | Lifton | Coryton | Lydford | Marytavy | Tavistock | Whitchurch Down Platform | Horrabridge | Yelverton | Shaugh Bridge Platform | Bickleigh | Plym Bridge Platform | Marsh Mills | Main / Tavist. / Junct.
— 4m. 53c. — 3m. 18c. — 4m. 33c. — 3m. 20c. — 3m. 32c. — 1m 6c. — 2m. 68c. — 1m. 40c. — 2m. 38c. — 70c. — 2m 50c. — 1m. 21c. — 18c. —
— 30m 67c. —

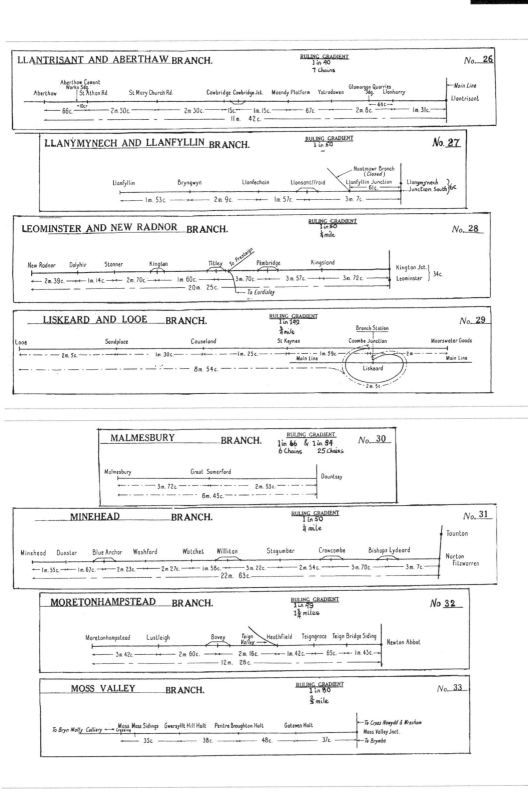

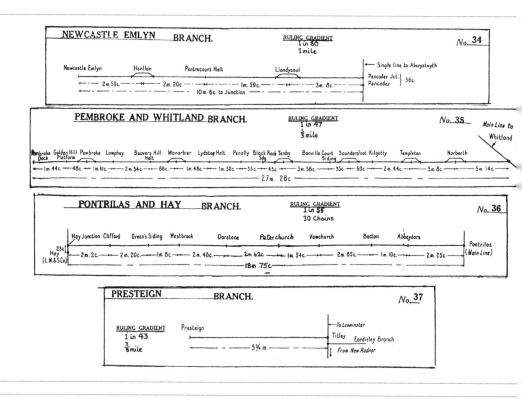

NEWCASTLE EMLYN BRANCH.

RULING GRADIENT
1 in 80
1 mile

No. 34

Newcastle Emlyn — Henllan — Pentrecourt Halt — Llandyssul

Single line to Aberystwyth
Pencader Jct.
Pencader

← 2m.59c. → ← 2m.20c. → ← 1m.59c. → ← 3m.8c. → 36c.
←————— 10m.6c. to Junction —————→

PEMBROKE AND WHITLAND BRANCH.

RULING GRADIENT
1 in 47
½ mile

No. 35

Main Line to Whitland

Pembroke Dock — Golden Hill Platform — Pembroke — Lamphey — Beavers Hill Halt — Manorbier — Lydstep Halt — Penally — Black Rock Sdg. — Tenby — Saundersfoot — Kilgetty — Templeton — Narberth

Bonville Court Siding

←1m.44c.→←48c.→←1m.41c.→← 2m.54c.→←66c.→← 1m.48c.→← 1m.50c.→←55c.→←43c.→← 3m.58c.→←35c.→←60c.→← 2m.44c.→← 3m.8c.→← 5m.14c.→
←————————————————— 27m.28c. —————————————————→

PONTRILAS AND HAY BRANCH.

RULING GRADIENT
1 in 55
10 Chains

No. 36

23c.
Hay
(L.M.&S.Co) — Hay Junction — Clifford — Green's Siding — Westbrook — Dorstone — Peterchurch — Vowchurch — Bacton — Abbeydore — Pontrilas (Main Line)

← 2m.2c. → ← 2m.20c. → ←1m.8c.→ ← 2m.46c. → ← 2m.62c. → ← 1m.54c. → ← 2m.65c. → ← 1m.10c. → ← 2m.25c. →
←————————————— 18m.75c. —————————————→

PRESTEIGN BRANCH.

No. 37

RULING GRADIENT
1 in 43
⅜ mile

Presteign

To Leominster
Titley — Eardisley Branch
From New Radnor

←————— 5¾ m. —————→

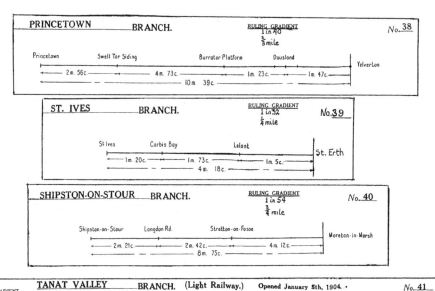

PRINCETOWN BRANCH.

RULING GRADIENT
1 in 40
⅔ mile

No. 38

Princetown — Swell Tor Siding — Burrator Platform — Dousland — Yelverton

← 2m.56c. → ← 4m.73c. → ← 1m.23c. → ← 1m.47c. →
←————————— 10m.39c. —————————→

ST. IVES BRANCH.

RULING GRADIENT
1 in 32
¼ mile

No. 39

St Ives — Carbis Bay — Lelant — St. Erth

← 1m.20c. → ← 1m.73c. → ← 1m.5c. →
←————— 4m.18c. —————→

SHIPSTON-ON-STOUR BRANCH.

RULING GRADIENT
1 in 54
¾ mile

No. 40

Shipston-on-Stour — Longdon Rd. — Stretton-on-Fosse — Moreton-in-Marsh

← 2m.21c. → ← 2m.42c. → ← 4m.12c. →
←————— 8m.75c. —————→

RULING GRADIENT
1 in 63
40 Chains

TANAT VALLEY BRANCH. (Light Railway.) Opened January 5th, 1904.

No. 41

Llangynog — Penybontfawr — Pedair Ffordd Halt — Llanrhaiadr Mochnant — Pentrefelin Halt — Llangedwyn — Llansilin Rd. — Glanyrafon Halt — Llanyblodwell Halt — Bladwell Jct.

Nantmawr Branch: 1m.18c.
Porthywaen Private Siding — Oswestry — Llynclys — Llynclys Jct.

Nantmawr Branch (closed)

←2m.43c.→←1m.57c.→←1m.8c.→← 1m.32c.→← 1m.70c.→← 1m.50c.→← 1m.19c.→← 1m.15c.→←56c.→← 1m.36c.→← 1m.4c.→ 17c.

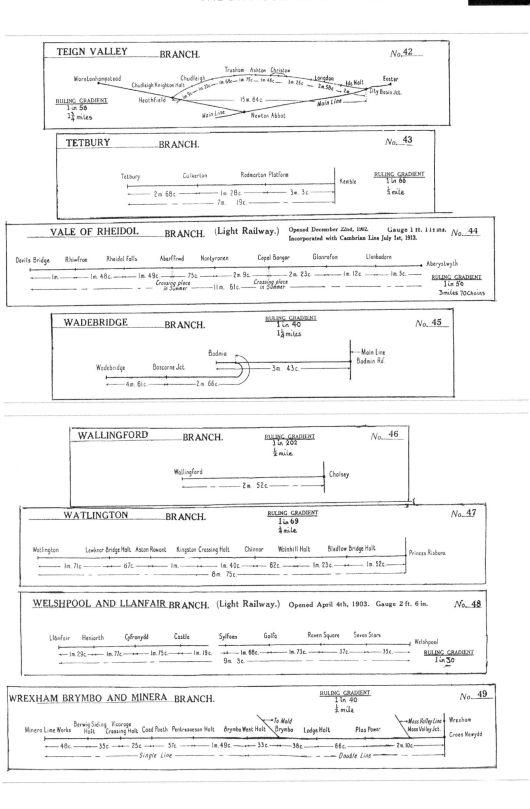

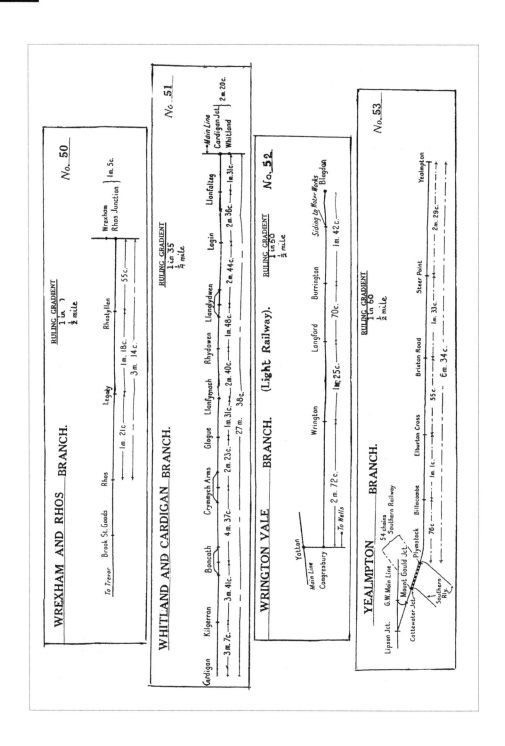

Ruling Gradients for some Early Steam Rail Motor Car Routes. (Source: PRO RAIL 937, PIECE 135)

	DOWN	UP		DOWN	UP
Plymouth	-	-	Chasewater	-	81F
Plymouth North Road	61R		Blackwater Jn E	72R	72F
Mutley	77R		Blackwater Jn N	60R	L
Lipson Vale H	72F		Stop Board		60F
Plymstock	66R	70F	Mount Hawke H	60R	112F
Billacombe	70R	68F	St Agnes	112F	60R
Elburton Xing	68R	60R	Stop Board	L	
Brixton Road	60F	60R	Goonbell H	60F	55R
Steer Point	60F	60F	Mithian H	55F	45R
Yealmpton	60R		Perranporth	45F	45F
Stonehouse		300F	Goonhaven H	45F	56F
Ebley Xing H	302R	276F	Stop Board		61R
Downfield Xing H	276R	272R	Shepherds	46R	45R
Stroud	234R	200R	Stop Board	264F	
Bowbridge Xing H	250R	250F	Mitchell & Newlyn H	45F	48R
Ham Mill Xing H	250R	250F	Trewerry & Trerice H	48F	110R
Brimscombe Bridge H	250R	185F	Trewerry Xing & Siding	224F	84F
Brimscombe	185R	75F	Trevemper Siding	84R	146R
St Mary's Crossing H	103R	70F	Tolcarn Junction	84R	146R
Chalford	70R		Newquay	146F	
Ivybridge		170R	Truro		60F
Cornwood	133F	150R	Penwithers Junction	60R	64F
Hemerdon Siding	160R	42R	Chasewater	61R	65F
Stop Board	L		Blackwater Junction E	65R	62F
Plympton	42F	81R	Wheal Busy Siding	69R	81R
Tavistock Junction	81F	L	Scorrier	81F	60F
Laira Junction	L	77F	Drump Lane	60R	80R
Laira H	77R	83F	Redruth	80F	112R
Lipson Junction	83R	83F	Redruth Junction	120F	337F
Lipson Vale H	83R	72F	Carn Brea Yard	337R	141R
Mannamead	72R	77R	Carn Brea	141F	161F
Mutley	72R	77R	N Crofty Junction	161F	349F
North Road	77F	66R	Dolcoach Siding	349R	122R
Cornwall Junction	66F	61R	Roskear Junction	122F	108R
Plymouth	61F	61F	Stop Board	108F	
Cornwall Junction	61R	55F	Camborne	82F	55R

	DOWN	UP		DOWN	UP
Devonport Junction	55R	100F	Gwinear Road	55F	61R
Devonport	59R	76R	Gwinear Road Stop Board	142F	
Dockyard H	515F	73R	Hayle	61F	70F
Ford H	515F	73R	St Erth	70R	67F
Keyham	73F	59R	Marazion	67R	191F
St Budeaux E	99R	59R	Long Rock	191R	L
St Budeaux Platform	99R	62F	Ponsandane Siding	L	L
St Budeaux W	99R	62F	Penzance	L	-
Royal Albert Bridge	62R	81R	Wrexham		200F
Saltash	81F	64R	Johnston & Havod		200R
Defiance Platform	64F	123R	Ruabon		334R
Wearde	101R	120F	Cefn		83R
St Germans	120R		Chirk		143F
Plymouth	-	61F	Preesgweene		140R
Plymouth North Road	61R	77F	Gobowen		156R
Mutley	77R	72R	Ruabon	75F	
Lipson Vale H	72F	83R	Llangollen Line Junction		341R
Laira H	83F	77R	Acrefair	75R	85R
Laira Junction	77F	L	Trevor	85F	75R
Tavistock Junction	L	100F	Llangollen	330R	80F
Marsh Mills	100R	97F	Berwyn	80R	435R
Lee Moor Xing	97R	60F	Gladyfrdwy	80R	352F
Plym Bridge Platform	60R	60F	Carrog	352R	300R
Bickleigh	60R	58F	Corwen	276 R	L
Shaugh Bridge Platf'rm	58R	58F	Cynnyd	200R	200R
Yelverton	58R	60R	Llandrillo	200R	200R
Horrabridge	60F	60R	Llandderfel	150R	300R
Whitch'rch Down P'frm	60F	165R	Bala Junction	150R	220R
Tavistock	165F	-	Llanwchllyn	71R	63F
Southall	-	102R	Drws-y-Nant	58F	50R
Trumpers Xing H	102F	110R	Bontnewydd	50F	91R
Brentford	110F	120R	Dogelley	91F	-

Gradients taken from '1912–24 Gradient Diagrams, Various Lines and Branches' (15 items) (Source: PRO RAIL 253, PIECE 689)

This document is nowhere near a collection of the complete GWR system, being just a random selection of a few main and branch lines. For the contents, see the note in the PRO Index between the pages listing the RAIL 253, PIECES 212 and 213. Items of Steam Rail Motor Car interest include the following:

BALA to DOLGELLEY   Sheet 66
RUABON to BALA   Sheet 65

Dolgelley was 40ft above sea level.

Three miles out of Dolgelley was Bont-Newydd (approx 175ft above sea level) where the line climbed at 1:50 for just under 1.5 miles.

6.5 miles out of Dolgelley was Drws-y-Nant (approx 485ft above sea level) where the line climbed for about 3 miles at gradients of 1:62, 65, 59 and 58 to the summit at about 750ft.

The line then fell to Llanuwchlly (approx 560ft above sea level) with gradients of 1:65 and 63. There followed a gradual drop to Berwyn Tunnel (approx 400ft above sea level), followed by a 1⅙-mile drop through Berwyn at 1:80, and on to Llangollen, (approx 250ft above sea level).

From Llangollen to Trevor   1 mile at 1:75 climbing
Trevor to Acrefair   1 mile at 1:85½ climbing
Acrefair to Ruabon   ¾ mile at 1:75 falling

A rough sketch of the gradient profile of these routes are in the hard copy.

SOUTHALL AREA

Nothing of importance.

PLYMPTON to DEFIANCE

Forder viaduct to Plymouth Millbay	– short sections 1:63 to 1:60
Mutley Tunnel through Laira Halt	– $1^{1}/_{3}$ miles dropping at 1:60
East of Plympton	– $^{2}/_{3}$ mile at 1:43 climbing

3. Statement of Curves, Gradients, Engines Used and Loads of Trains on Branch Lines, etc 1902 (PRO RAIL 253, PIECE 288)

This is a small booklet of limited use but includes the following:

Under 'Maximum Gradients'

Rising 1:50 for Llangollen for 'up' journey, i.e. to Ruabon – Falling 1:54¾ for 'down' journey.

Victoria Line 1:60 – West London Junction to North Pole Junction 'up' journey (direction with Main Line), 34 chains

Minera 'up' journey	Rising 669	: Falling 30
Rhos	Rising …	: Falling 50

CONTENTS - INDEX

1. RULING GRADIENTS FOR SOME EARLY STEAM RAIL MOTOR CAR ROUTES
SOURCE P.R.O. RAIL937 PIECE 135

2. GRADIENTS TAKEN FROM "1912 - 1924 GRADIENT DIAGRAMS, VARIOUS
LINES AND BRANCHES" (15 ITEMS) P.R.O. RAIL 253 PIECE 689

STATEMENT OF CURVES, GRADIENTS, ENGINES USED AND LOADS OF
TRAINS ON BRANCH LINES, ETC. 1902 (P.R.O. RAIL 253 PIECE 288)

TEXT

1. RULING GRADIENTS FOR SOME EARLY STEAM RAIL MOTOR CAR ROUTES
SOURCE P.R.O. RAIL937 PIECE 135   July PCC Sept 1923

Station	DOWN	UP
Plymouth		
North Road	-	61R
Mutley	77R	77F
Lipson Vale H.	72F	L
Plymstock	66R	70F
Billacombe	70R	68F
Elburton Xing	68R	60R
Brixton Road	60F	60R
Steer Point	60F	60F
Yealmpton	60R	
Stonehouse		
Ebley Xing H.	302R	300F
Downfield Xing H.	276R	276F
Stroud	234R	272R
Bowbridge Xing H.	250R	200R
Ham Mill Xing H.	250R	250F
Brimscombe Bridge H.	250R	250F
Brimscombe	250R	185R
Siding	185R	75F
St.Mary's Crossing H.	103R	
Chalford	70R	70F
Ivybridge	133F	170R
Cornwood	150R	150R

Station	DOWN	UP
Chasewater		
Blackwater Jn.E.	-	81F
" N.	72F	72F
Stop Board	60R	L
Mount Hawke H.	60R	60F
St.Agnes	112F	112R
Stop Board	L	60R
Goonbell H.	60R	55R
Mithian H.	55F	45R
Perranporth	45F	45F
Goonhaven H.	45F	56F
Stop Board	-	61R
Shepherds	46R	45R
Stop Board	264F	
Mitchell & Newlyn H.	45F	48R
Trewerry & Trerice H.	48F	
Trewerry Xing & Siding	224F	110R
Trevemper Siding		84F
Tolcarn Jn.	84R	146R
Newquay	146F	146R
Truro		
Penwithers Jn.	60R	60F
		64F

Hemerdon Sdng.	160R		42R
Stop Board	L		
Plympton	42F	42F	81R
Tavistock Jn.	81R	81R	L
Laira Jn.	L	L	77F
Laira H.	77R	77F	83F
Lipson Jn.	83R	83F	83F
Lipson Vale H.	83R	72F	72F
Mannamead	72R	77R	77R
Mutley	72R	77R	77R
North Road	77F	66R	66R
Cornwall Jn.	66R	61F	61R
Plymouth	61F	61R	61F
Cornwall Jn.	61R	55F	55F
Devonport Jn.	55R	100F	100F
Devonport	59R	76R	76R
Dockyard H.	76F	170R	170R
Ford H.	515F	73R	73R
Keyham	73F	59R	59R
St.Budeaux E.	59R	59R	59R
St.Budeaux Platf'm	99R	62F	62F
St.Budeaux W.	99R	62F	62F
R.Albert Bridge	62R	81R	81R
Saltash	81F	64R	64R
Defiance Platform	64F	123R	123R
Wearde	101R	120F	
St.Germans	120R		

Plymouth			
North Road	-	61R	61R
Mutley	61R	77R	77F
Lipson Vale H.	77R	72F	72R
Laira H.	72F	83R	83R
Laira Jn.	83R	77F	77R
Tavistock Jn.	77F	L	L
Marsh Mills	L	100R	100F
Lee Moor Xing	100R	97R	97F
Plym Bridge Plat.	97R	60R	60F
Bickleigh	60R	60R	60F
Shaugh Bridge Plat.	58R	58F	58F
Yelverton	58R	60R	60R
Horrabridge	60F	60F	
Whitchurch Down Platform		L	75F
Tavistock	60F	165R	
	165F	-	

Chasewater	61R	65F
Blackwater Jn.E.	65R	62F
Wheal Busy Sdng.	69R	81R
Scorrier	81F	60F
Drump Lane	60R	80R
Redruth	80F	113R
Redruth Jn.	120F	337F
Carn Brea Yard	337R	141R
Carn Brea	141F	161F
N. Crofty Jn.	161R	349F
Dolcoath Sdng.	349R	122R
Roskear Jn.	122F	108R
Stop Board	108F	
Camborne	82F	55R
Gwinear Road	55F	61R
Gwinear Road St'p Board	142F	
Hayle	61F	70F
St.Erth	70R	67F
Marazion	67R	191R
Long Rock	191R	L
Ponsandane Sdng.	L	L
Penzance	L	-

Wrexham	200F	200F
Johnston & Havod	200R	200R
Ruabon	334R	334R
Cefn	83R	83R
Chirk	143F	143F
Preesgweene	140R	140R
Goboven	156R	156R

Ruabon		75F
Llangollen Line Jn.		
Acrefair	100R	341R
Trevor	97R	85R
Llangollen	60R	75R
Berwyn	60R	330R
Glandyfrdwy	58R	80R
Carrog	60R	435R
Corwen	276R	352F
Cynnyd	200R	300R
Llandrillo	200R	L
Llanderfel	150R	200R
Bala Jn.	150R	300R
Llanwchllyn	71R	220R
Drws-y-Nant	58F	63F
Bontnewydd	50F	50R
Dolgelley	91F	91R
		-

Southall	-	102R
Trumpers Xing H.	102F	110R
Brentford	110F	120R

2. GRADIENTS TAKEN FROM "1912 - 1924 GRADIENT DIAGRAMS, VARIOUS LINES AND BRANCHES" (15 ITEMS) P.R.O. RAIL 253 PIECE 689

This document is nowhere near a collection of the complete G.W.R. system, being just a random selection of a few main and branch lines. For the contents, see the note in the P.R.O. INDEX between the pages listing the RAIL 253 PIECES 212 and 213. Items of Steam Rail Motor Car interest include the following:-

BALA TO DOLGELLEY SHEET 66
RUABON TO BALA SHEET 65
Dolgelley was 40 feet above sea level.
Three miles out of Dolgelley was Bont-Newydd (approximately 175 feet above sea level) where the line climbed at 1 in 50 for just under one and a half miles.
Six and a half miles out of Dolgelley was Drws-y-Nant (approximately 485 feet above sea level) where the line climbed for about three miles at gradients of 1 in 62, 65, 59 and 58 to the summit at about 750 feet.
The line then fell to Llanuwchllyn (approximately 560 feet above sea level) with gradients of 1 in 65 and 63. There followed a gradual drop to Berwyn Tunnel (approximately 400 feet above sea level), followed by a one and one sixth miles drop through Berwyn at 1 in 80, and on to Llangollen, (approximately 250 feet above sea level).
From Llangollen to Ruabon the gradients were as follows:-

Llangollen to Trevor	One mile at 1 in 75 climbing
Trevor to Acrefair	One mile at 1 in 85½ climbing
Acrefair to Ruabon	three-quarters of a mile at 1 in 75 falling

A rough sketch of the gradient profile of these routes are in the hard copy.

SOUTHALL AREA
Nothing of importance

PLYMTON TO DEFIANCE
Forder viaduct to Plymouth Millbay - short sections 1 in 63 to 1 in 60
Mutley Tunnel through Laira Halt - one and one third miles dropping at 1 in 60
East of Plympton - two-thirds of a mile at 1 in 43 climbing

STATEMENT OF CURVES, GRADIENTS, ENGINES USED AND LOADS OF TRAINS ON BRANCH LINES, ETC. 1902 (P.R.O. RAIL 253 PIECE 288)

This is a small booklet of limited use but includes the following:

Under "Maximum Gradients"
Rising 1 in 50 for Llangollen for "up" journey, i.e. to Ruabon
Falling 1 in 54½ for "down" journey
Victoria line 1 in 60 - West London Junction to North Pole Junction "up" journey (direction of junction with Main Line), 34 chains
Minera "up" journey Rising 669, Falling 30
Rhos   Rising .... Falling 50

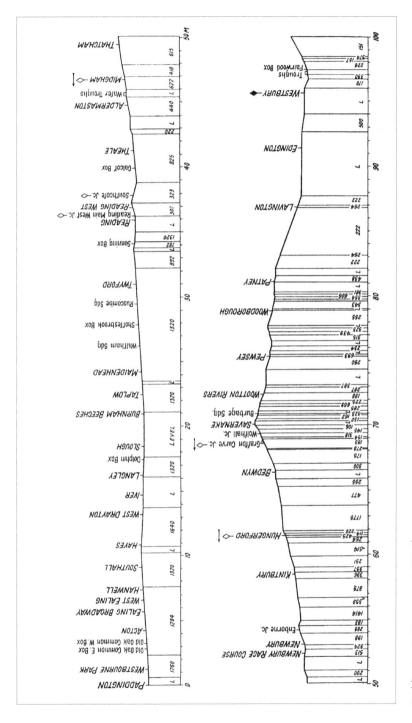

Paddington to Penzance via Westbury.

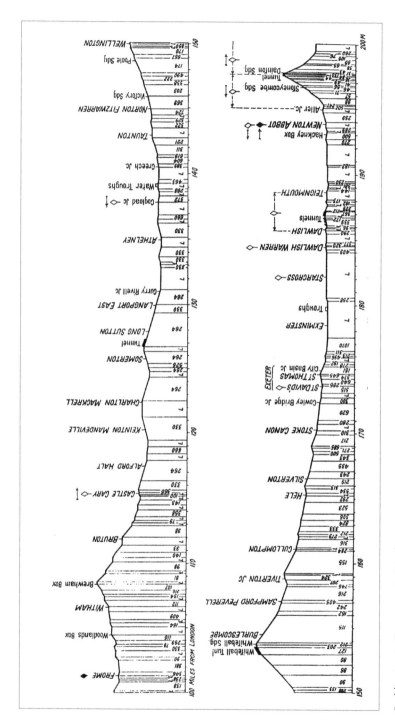

Paddington to Penzance via Westbury.

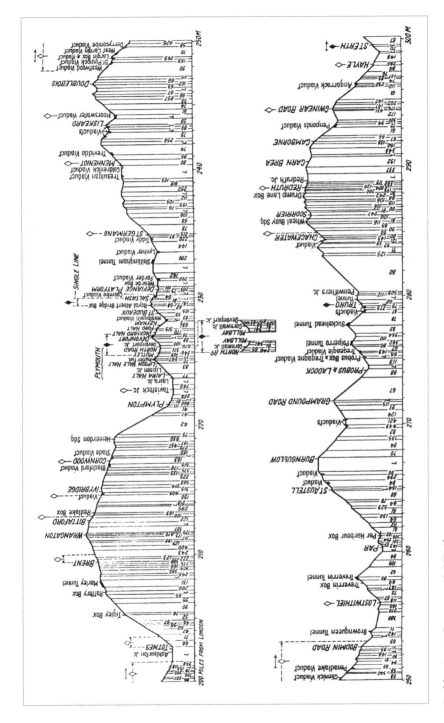

Paddington to Penzance via Westbury.

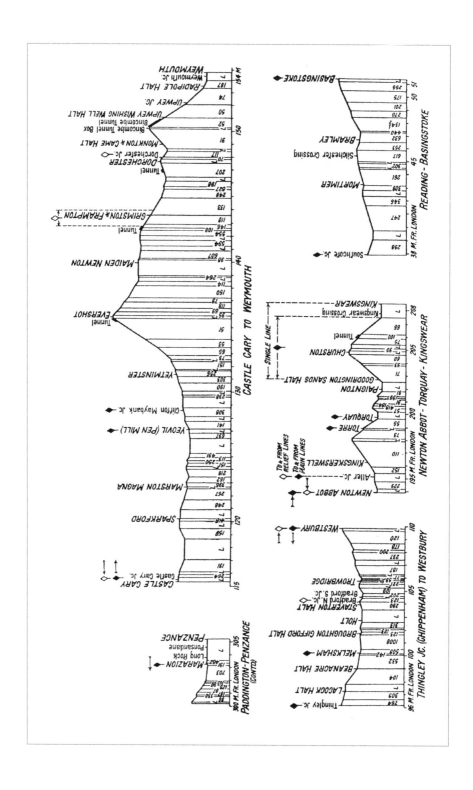

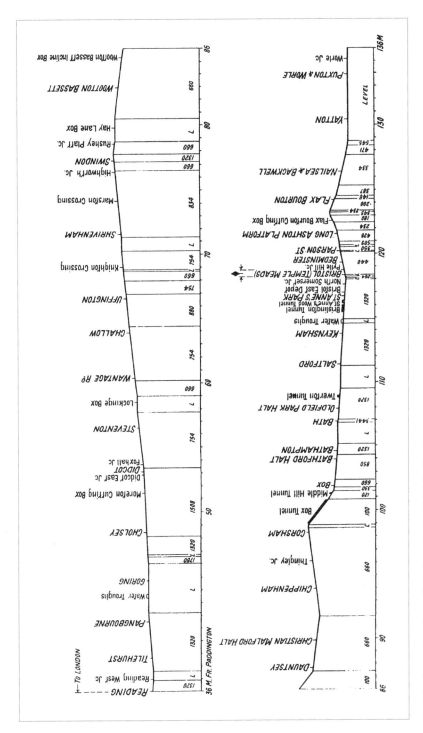

(Paddington) – Reading – Swindon – Bath – Bristol – Taunton.

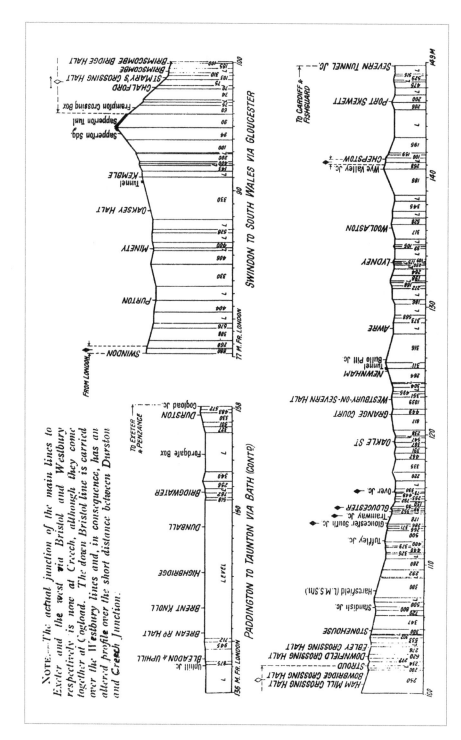

NOTE.—The actual junction of the main lines to Exeter and the west via Bristol and Westbury respectively is none at Creech, although they come together at Cogload. The down Bristol line is carried over the Westbury lines and, in consequence, has an altered profile over the short distance between Durston and Creech Junction.

PADDINGTON TO TAUNTON VIA BATH (CONT'D)

SWINDON TO SOUTH WALES VIA GLOUCESTER

SWINDON TO SOUTH WALES VIA GLOUCESTER (CONT'D)

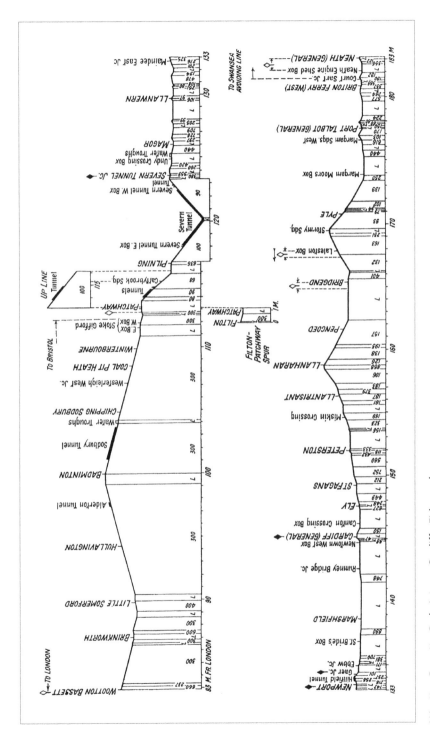

Wootton Bassett – Badminton – Cardiff – Fishguard

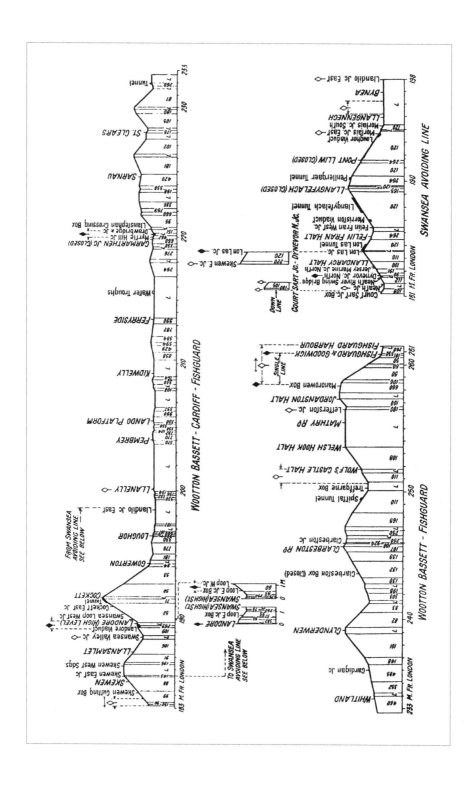

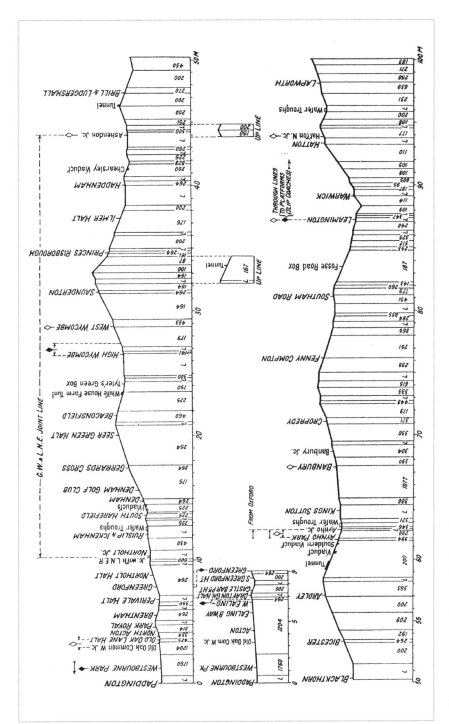

Paddington to Birmingham and Chester (via Bicester).

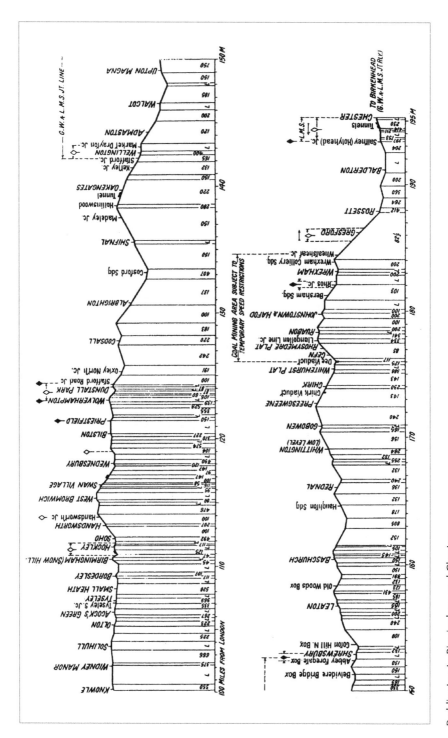

Paddington to Birmingham and Chester.

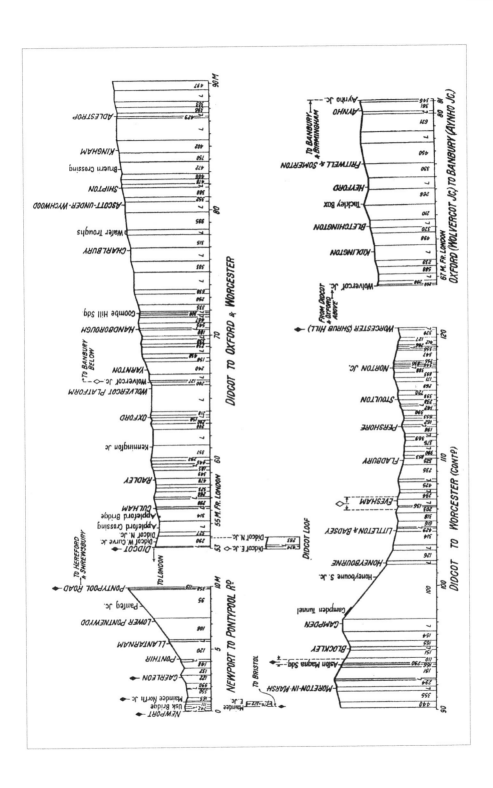

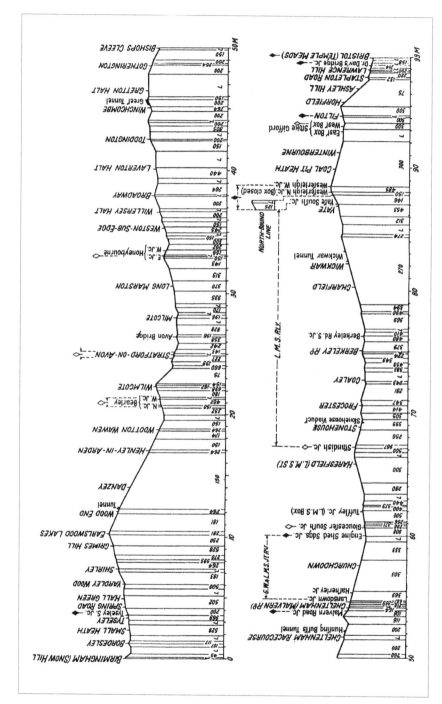

Birmingham to Stratford-on-Avon, Cheltenham and Bristol.

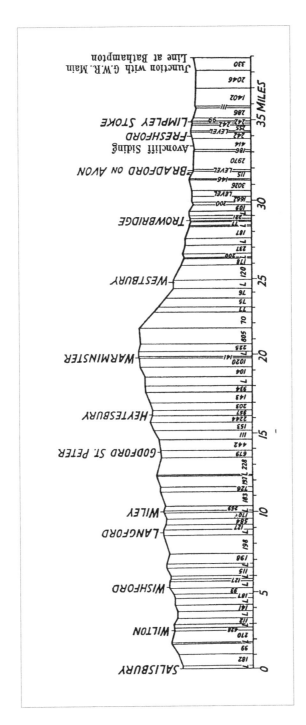

Salisbury – Bathampton.

8

THE WILKINSON REPORT OF 1925

A Branch Line Analysis

The 1922/23 Amalgamation, while it nominally formed the 'Big Four', GWR, LNER, LMS and SR, really did nothing for the GWR. The GWR, while maybe gaining technically, gained really nothing of advantage, having absorbed anything profitable years before. The only gain, if such it could be termed, was a mass of motive power and other rolling stock ranging in condition from excellent to 'Where's the nearest scrap yard?', virtually nothing to GWR standards and components.

In the prevailing conditions of the early 1920s, following on the heels of the 1914–18 war, economies were being sought countrywide, and cuts would soon be proposed in every industry. Thus in the mid 1920s, the GWR Assistant Superintendent of the line, F. Wilkinson, was instructed to examine and report on the potential for extended use of the rail motor concept and on the viability of branch lines on the system, thus pre-empting by a quarter century the 'slash and burn' policy of Dr Beeching.

F. Wilkinson's terms of reference were:

1. Are branch lines being worked today on the most economical lines and is the present system capable of improvement?
2. How far would it meet the case to abolish steam locomotives and our heavy rolling stock and substitute a motorrail coach with a light trailer for goods and luggage; and, on which lines would this be possible, for it is realised that not all branch lines are alike? [Author's note: this must have caused some raised eyebrows!]
3. Is there any case in which the rails could be taken up and the road used as a motor road by the Company, in which case possibly one man in charge of the station would be adequate to attend to tickets and goods?

Thus was expressed a hope that by expanding the use of the motor railcar, possibly to a different design to that existing, savings would inevitably accrue as the heavier rolling stock had been eliminated.

Preliminary inspections were undertaken and showed that there were two types of 'branch' lines, both with individual requirements. These were:

1. Branches that are self contained and are worked by services that entail a change for passengers at a junction station, there being a through connection for goods traffic only.
2. Branches served by trains, auto services or rail motors that work between the branch and the local businesses, shopping or market centre on the main line.
    (Not strictly a 'branch' but similar operational requirements.)

At this time, around 1925, it had long been recognised that many of the branch and main-line halts and smaller stations were at some considerable distance from the villages and hamlets they nominally served. Recognised also was the burgeoning use of road motor transport, which, taking the country roads, was much quicker and more convenient for passengers who would have used the train. So it was that the lines built when the railway was the only alternative to the horse were at a disadvantage to start with.

In addition to rail motors, the ordinary locomotive and the auto engine (the latter an ordinary engine controllable from the towed trailer car) were all employed on the system. While in the early years, the flush of enthusiasm for the rail motor had predicted great economies, it was found in practice that, in many cases, sole use of the rail motor was not possible due to the nature of loads to be picked up in addition to passengers, and thus the two other classifications of motive power was a must. The latter engines could also be detached, when lightly used, and employed on other duties such as shunting, and were quite capable of light goods trains of horse boxes, milk wagons and so on, for which a steam rail motor is not really suited, nor indeed in some cases powerful enough.

Thus Report paragraph 16 reads:

Rail motors are in use on a limited number of branches where circumstances are favourable, but they are unsuited for general use on branches. Like ordinary engines and auto engines, they entail the employment of two enginemen, and whilst they have a low coal consumption, are only capable of conveying a very limited number of additional vehicles (including horse boxes and milk trucks), which are dealt with on all branches at times. Further, a rail motor cannot work a goods train, is not adapted for shunting, and has difficulty in getting up steep gradients, which are common on branches. Where rail motors are used for passenger services, a mainline engine works over the branch to pick up or put off goods traffic.

This comment was followed by paragraph 17:

> Whilst rail motors are useful for supplementing purely passenger carrying services, they may be regarded as generally unsuitable for use on branch lines: the same remark applies to vehicles of similar type i.e. Sentinel-Cammell rail cars, petrol cars and petrol/electric cars.

At this time it must have been generally accepted that rail motors were not really as economic as had been predicted, as in the country as a whole only ninety-one rail motors were now in use, fifty-three of them being on the GWR, thus demonstrating their unsuitability for general railway use but still fighting a rearguard action on the GWR.

Other economies were being examined, and branch-line signalling was also under scrutiny. As outlined in the Rail motor Routes section, with two exceptions, the branches were all single line and were worked under one of the Ministry of Transport train 'staff' systems. The recommendations included the closing of some signal boxes, following a further check on the practical expedient of using power from a main-line box to operate branch points. In this case, which seems rather antiquated today, it was suggested that the signalman could operate a 'hand generator' for a few seconds to initiate the required point movement.

One box proposed for closure was the West Drayton loop box, which worked the Staines branch points and was to have its 'staff' pillar attached to the station and not in the signal box, from which the station staff would extract the 'staff' (confusing nomenclature isn't it?) on electrical instruction from the signalman. There was also a move to dispense with the services of 'flagmen' when branch single line repairs were to be undertaken. The driver would be supplied with the usual speed restriction notice so it was up to the driver, the flagman being thus available for actual repair assistance on the track. Further cuts were recommended in the use of electrical signalling equipment thus reducing maintenance and staffing costs. Selected branches using the electric tablet, staff or token were to have the system removed and the trains rescheduled to suit. These were: Blenheim, Bridport (between Bridport and West Bay), Clynderwen and Letterston (between Letterston and Letterston Junction), Cardigan and Whittand (instruments removed at Llanfaltey), Leominster and New Radnor (between Kington and New Radnor), Wrexham and Rhos (between Rhos and Brook Street), Wrexham, Brymbo and Minera (between Coed Poeth and Berwig), Moss Valley Line, Tetbury Branch, Liskeard and Looe Line (between Coombe Junction and Looe).

No stone was to be unturned to obtain savings, and one recommendation was the reduction of the number of telegraph poles when pole renewal was due, and running the wires along the boundary fences! A further economy was suggested with the latter, to the extent that certain selected track sections did not need fences anyway, and should not be renewed. Little used sidings should also be closely examined and removed from service.

A strong suggestion was included that some branches should be re-designated as light railways. It was acknowledged that there were some disadvantages, including reduced speed running and the requirement of lighting and cattle guards at unmanned level crossings. To counter these, it was noted that advantages could include dispensing with gatekeepers, gates and signalling equipment at public level crossings, a not inconsiderable expense. It was also noted that a review of accounting procedures should be made with a view to combining and simplifying clerical and supervisory duties, all with a view to reducing staff.

Certain branches were recommended for closure, and these were Yealmpton, Llantrisant and Aberthaw (between Cowbridge and Aberthaw), Eardsley, Dinas Mawddwy, Pontrilas and Hay, Welshpool and Llanfair. Branch-line working hours were to be reduced to eight on the Cleobury Mortimer and Ditton Priors, and the Vale of Reidol.

Transfer of passengers to road services was recommended at Pontrilas and Hay, Tanat Valley Line, Hemyock Branch, Mon Valley Line, Abermule and Kerry. There was also a recommendation for obtaining a Sentinel-type rail motor (this was not a Sentinel-Cammell rail car), for trial on the 'lighter branch lines effecting economy in coal and wages', but there appears to be no reference to this actually being done from the Superintendent's and managerial reports of the period.

Having acknowledged the difficulties with steam rail motors and additional trailer vehicles and vans, and also acknowledging the Sentinel-Cammell rail coach was unsuitable for such use, the Sentinel Wagon Company had 'produced an engine as a separate unit which appears to be a very economical machine'. Wilkinson and a representative of Mr Collett had been impressed by their inspection of such an engine. Coal consumption under normal running conditions was noted as 10lbs/mile, whereas a GWR rail motor consumed 20.4lbs/mile minimum and could be as high as 56lbs/mile. This was probably an unfair comparison in respect of varied running conditions and standing time, but it was nevertheless impressive in terms of bald figure comparisons.

A further controversial saving was the fact that the Sentinel engine could be worked by one man. Objections could be expected on the grounds of safety, which always raises its head, even or more under current Health and

Safety Regulations, but an example use of a Sentinel by the Derwent Valley Light Railway was noted. Displacing a usual type engine, running expenses had been cut from £2,915 in 1924 to £1,357 in 1925, hauling a train of three four-wheeled coaches weighing 42 tons and carrying 150 passengers, with a ruling gradient of 1:150 occurring at several stretches of the line.

As well as the Sentinel-Cammell powered railcar, sales of which had now reached a large number, shunters were also produced. The cars themselves had now reached the far corners of the earth, including such places as Peru, Egypt, Tasmania, Paraguay and Ceylon, in eight formats ranging from 100 to 400hp, and in gauges of 2ft 6in to 5ft 6in. As well as the standard sales versions there were several experimental (but not overly successful) designs. While the GWR was having second thoughts on their use, other countries were stocking up.

It would appear to be the separate shunter version that Mr Wilkinson and Collett's representatives went to examine. These also had a wide market and had a somewhat unique design, at least in terms of the usual GWR steam rail motor design of power unit. The superheated boiler worked at 275psi pressure and was fed downward through the centre flue. Vertical cylinders (6¾in x 9in) drove a 500rpm crankshaft by means of chains and sprockets, and drive ratios could be varied depending on the work the engine was required to do. For very heavy work, an additional gearwheel could be keyed to mesh with a spur gear between the crankshaft and the countershaft onto which were keyed the drive sprockets.

All of the shunters had four wheels, and on the larger 200hp versions, the standard engine unit was just doubled up. Steam was supplied by a 100hp or a larger 200hp boiler, both being water-tube not fire-tube designs. There was also an interesting braking arrangement. In addition to the usual hand and steam brakes, a unique arrangement of drawing air into the cylinders and compressing it to form a 'retarder' was installed, exhausting by means of a foot pedal. However impressive, management appears to have quietly shelved the Sentinel recommendation.

The Report concluded with an analysis of recommendations outlined, with a summary of savings if all were applied to the fifty-three branch lines (listed in Chapter 6). £64,208 was the figure quoted, but underlying the report, bearing in mind its instigation in the first place, i.e. the potential for spreading the use of the steam rail motor, the hammer-blow was struck by paragraphs 75 to 77 of the Report:

> A Rail motor Car…Steam, Petrol or Petrol Electric…would have difficulty in hauling extra vehicles (on the gradients of most branches). A Steam Engine would still have to be employed to lift heavier traffic… Rail motors are not

altogether satisfactory in working. The engine is liable to failure and when it or the passenger portion of the car requires attention the whole vehicle is placed out of use.

Paragraph 77 plainly states:

Under the circumstances which obtain on the Company's Branch lines, the proposal to employ Rail motors with goods trailers would not meet requirements.

Thus in these blunt terms one of the final nails was prepared for the existing rail motor's coffin, but, with management probably a little nonplussed by the very negative conclusion on a proposal which, like many others, 'seemed a good idea at the time', the railcar problem slumbered on in a diminishing field, only to pop up again three years later.

At the January 1927 Superintendents Meeting, the need to increase revenue was still a major topic, and a proposal was put forward, (the whole idea seemed to be a sort of clutching-at-any-straw-to-survive!) to utilise the back of the rail motor tickets for advertising purposes, but after considerable discussion the decision to not recommend was made on the grounds that such advertising may antagonise some of the other companies with which the GWR did business.

In spite of the negative signal emanating from the 1925 Wilkinson Report on the future of branch lines and the ineffectiveness of the steam rail motor, or indeed any design of rail motor, February 1928 heralded yet another rail motor proposal. The continuing and rapid expansion of road transport was still causing even greater concern, and efforts to counter its spread were the orders of the day. Among the proposals came one for yet another rail motor! The design was to be of special light construction, with a capacity of forty passengers without the usual accommodation for luggage, and 'similar in type and equipment to road buses'. A quick acceleration was required and the capacity to maintain a speed of 35mph. The propelling system was to be steam, oil or petrol, with a leaning toward ease of access from the 'low ballast' rural platforms. There was also the insistence that the mileage costs had to be below that of the existing rail motors. The vehicle was to be utilised 'in a place of or in addition to, existing or branch line services wherever traffic can be secured, but not to convey rail traffic'. Route proposals were to be forwarded for consideration when more detailed information became available, concerning design and capacity of the new vehicle.

At the end of 1928, whilst the proposal was still being mulled over, a note is recorded that 'there are ten steam rail motors currently at Swindon and classified as spare'. A request was then put forward for any ideas where, or if, they could be used before conversion to trailer cars. There appeared to be no ideas forthcoming so conversion proceeded.

The suggestion of the February 1928 meeting was to bear fruit several years later when No. 1 Diesel Mechanical Railcar entered service on 4 December 1933 in the Reading area. Thirty-eight were to be added between 1933 and 1941, the successors to steam, although not in the same numbers, but that is a different story.

The Wilkinson Report had thus finally put the cap on the steam rail motor venture and started the beginning of the end of a segment, quite unique in its way, of GWR history.

The Wilkinson Report was not the only feature of closures. Between 1923 and Nationalisation of 1947, a sequence of closures of branch lines stretched on into the 1940s, thirty-four being closed up to 1940 itself for passenger traffic. During this period, *new* stations and halts are listed totalling 111.

Again in the 1923–47 period, many stations and halts were closed by the GWR, some to goods traffic (thirty-five), some to passengers (164), with some closed to goods and passengers at different dates, and 110 closed entirely.

This was completed during a clash regarding the fairness, or otherwise, of financial arrangements between expanding road haulage and the railway generally, with the railway companies demanding a fairer approach by government. With supporters for and against, the whole was dwarfed by arrangements for the cover required or anticipated for the looming 1939–45 war, but rumbled ineffectually on.

The branch lines over which the steam rail motors had run were further slashed in 1963 when Lord Beeching followed in the footsteps of Wilkinson, as shown on the map following.

The GW Area Showing the Branch Lines Closed by Beeching Cuts of 1963

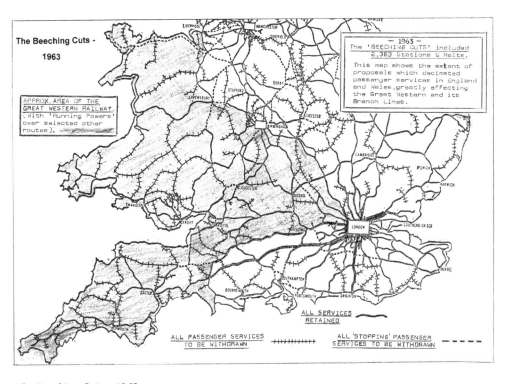

The Beeching Cuts – 1963.

9

THE STEAM RAIL MOTOR PROJECT: A 'LAST' OR 'FIRST' CHAPTER!

Although forming, as it does, the last chapter of this book, it is by no means the last chapter in the life and demise of the GWR's steam rail motor fleet.

There are, then, the opening lines of a new and exciting continuation of the steam rail motor story. The particular car involved, No. 93, converted in 1934 to trailer car No. 212, is the sole survivor of the fleet. In 1998, car No. 93 formed the centrepiece of a short ceremony at Didcot Great Western Rail Centre for the launch of the scheme to rebuild it into an operating steam rail motor once again, albeit eighty years 'down the line' from its birth, and after the chequered early working career.

After use as a trailer well into the 1940s, the now obsolete vehicle was sent into the workshops around 1954/5 for conversion to an office complex of four offices, two each side of the central vestibule, and retaining the end driving compartments for storage and the inevitable tea-making facilities. As mentioned in the preamble, the car stayed for about eighteen months at Swindon against the buffers of the track length outside the Carriage & Wagon offices, and was then moved, with the staff, to Reading, around 1958 (see plate 101). It was then parked, once again, against buffer stops on the bridge approach, the London side of Reading station.

The car stayed at this location for about eighteen months when it was once again moved to the Works at Wolverhampton, via the Worcester Carriage & Wagon shops where it was examined and serviced to maintain its 'mobile' classification. The author was at Wolverhampton for about a year, when he became Area Assistant and then handed over the coach to his successor, as his area became the Southwest and Wales. He then returned to Swindon where duties included redesign of the Diesel Fuel Injection repair shop, and another fascinating job, the rehash and re-equipment of the non-ferrous foundry (which stood him in good stead for involvement with the rebuild of the steam rail motor that kept him out of mischief during retirement!).

To return to the rail motor; after a period at Wolverhampton and in line with the fate of other railway works, the coach became one of the assets of the now closed Wolverhampton Works, 1 June 1964 seeing the end of yet another phase of railway history. Having been removed from service, what would now happen to it? Probably because of what it was, or had been, an enquiry triggered a report to the SVR Rolling Stock Committee regarding the condition of trailer car No. 079014, which had by now found its way to Lawley Street Goods Yard. The report on the vehicle was probably the most damning report that any committee would wish to receive. The Carriage & Wagon Inspector BR(M) (who would certainly wish to remain anonymous) forwarded a list of 'faults' which comprised the complete vehicle, in fact you name it and he'd condemned it (an ex-GWR vehicle examined by a Midland Region Inspector!). He criticised corrosion of the underframe (which was only his opinion as he couldn't have the body lifted off the frame), the bogies (spares unobtainable), the bogie frames (liable to cracking), obsolete draw gear (worn below minimum size), no brake cylinders or brake gear (spares unobtainable and prohibitively costed for manufacture). Body stripped out to provide office accommodation and roof damaged by leakage, and decaying 'due to lack of paint'. The vehicle, being 'completely out of gauge' with regard to height and width for movement out of the area under electric wires meant a roundabout route to destination at prohibitive cost. He then went into a lengthy dialogue on the dangers of stabling an unbraked vehicle, 'A lapse of staff memory could easily produce a runaway and injuries could result from an unstoppable vehicle on a siding … '

It was thus that, along with several other vehicles with equally damning reports, the SVR rejected the lot. Irrespective of the report in 1970, the coach was obtained by the Great Western Society with a view to preservation. Then followed a period of hibernation while it was decided how this unique vehicle could fit into the Great Western Society financial and rebuild programme. It was to be rather a long wait, in the interim being used for various purposes at Didcot, including overnight accommodation for 'Work Week' volunteers, etc. The intention when obtained by the Society along with other items was for sometime in the future to repair it and return it possibly to service as a rail motor but certainly to service as a trailer car. Having its obvious pedigree firmly in mind, however, the thought germinated: 'Having been a steam rail motor, what if…?'. What a unique rebuild programme that would make.

The rail motor rebuilding proposal eventually came to the top of the list, and an inaugural meeting was held at Didcot on 8 June 1993 between those technical and administration staff who would be the controlling faction if the venture was to succeed. Those attending this first meeting were: Messrs Croucher, Horwood, Howells, Hosegood, Tutton, Rudge and Knowles, each of whom had a specific skill or expertise in his own subject, all relevant to the programme. Costs for a 'one-off' proposal are far more than needed for a production run, and a figure of £400,000 appeared as acceptable for the project and seems an amazing amount considering the £2,100 cost new. Dr Ralph Tutton had produced a preliminary comprehensive document which outlined the possible requirements and sequence of events required for a successful rebuild programme and it was agreed that two groups would be formed, one for work on the 'coach work' and one for the engineering of the engine unit, the latter to be rebuilt from scratch as nothing currently existed. From the choice of fuels, i.e. gas, oil or coal, it was decided to follow the originals and stay with coal firing.

The search was on for any and all technical detail that may exist tucked away in archive corners or private collections, with visits proposed to all likely sites, including contacting the Manager of the Brecon Mountain Railway for a look at engine fittings etc. thought to match requirements. Mike Rudge, as engineer with extensive experience, undertook the drawing office requirement of preparing the component drawings from any information forthcoming. Roger Horwood and John Hosegood undertook the detailed examination of car No. 212, after its long sojourn on a siding awaiting attention.

In addition to the problems of obtaining technical information to assist with any proposed rebuild of the rail motor, there were other critical hurdles to overcome. Mentioned in the technical section of this book are the relevant material specifications when the vehicle was originally built. Technology has since advanced in leaps and bounds and the standards applied to material structures have changed in many ways in the intervening years, and new standards now apply.

The biggest hurdle comes in the form of the Railway Inspectorate, from whom very detailed permission must be obtained before anything can be done. It would be of no use to gear up everything to rebuild No. 93 if the Inspectorate said no! There are major facets governing rebuilding any old vehicle, or conversely building a completely new vehicle to an old design. With car No. 93 both facets were applicable as it would contain 'something old and something new'. The power bogie would be a completely new structure, requirements complicated by the need for a new boiler. This latter would be complicated further by modern 'pressure vessel' regulations, both for materials and methods of construction. The original boiler would have been a completely riveted structure, but modern techniques include welding, many boilers being now so constructed and such welding methods now strictly controlled. The major problem was felt to be the car body itself. It was very important to ensure that the Inspectorate understood that the *original* body existed in such a state that it could be repaired, and was in no sense a new construction. Modern carriages are to contain virtually no wood, have more than two exit/entrance doors and no 'tip over' form of tram seats. The structural frame of No. 93 was just all of these things. The underframe, while quite adequate for its purpose and repairable, would also not meet current construction regulations. Emphasis therefore had to be stressed that the body was a repair to an original vehicle and was in no way a new vehicle. A wooden vehicle with a coal fire in one end, and loaded with passengers, could give the Inspectorate nightmares. Pleading 'custom and practice' does not hold the weight it did!

All of the above fell exactly into the force of the Railway and other Transport Systems (Approval of Works, Plant and Equipment) Regulations 1994. The regulations came into force on 5 April 1994 and working with the Inspectorate is the only way to succeed. An exchange of all relevant documents thus continued and proposals were formulated along the strictest of guidelines, recently considerably tightened in the light of railway events.

So the long feasibility study was now officially off and running, its continuation dependent on available information and the amount of work required on the car body. All was of course reliant on funding and Richard Croucher, with financial and banking experience, was to manage the financial side of the project, while Dennis Howells, with extensive steam-engineering knowledge, was to be responsible for the 'engineering' requirement of the completely new power bogie.

During 1994, a couple of meetings on 22 March and 22 June outlined the continued search for information and construction drawings, and contained a preliminary note that the car should be under cover and that it would probably require a completely new body. There were also preliminary thoughts that building both power bogie and the car should be 'off site', i.e. away from Didcot.

The 4 October meeting reversed the building proposal and included acceptance of the need for workshop facilities to house the car on-site at Didcot. This latter of course adding to the cost estimates. The several site visits and information 'digs' had proved only partially successful so searching continued, and fund-raising was still a cause for concern. Extensive research by Dr Ralph Tutton allowed him to present a very detailed report to the committee on 13 June 1995, outlining a procedure plan and listing sources (known at the time) of available drawings. With the latter it was also proving difficult to recruit draftsmen to assist with such requirements when official drawings no longer existed. Certain information was available, however, and it was agreed that the frames for the power bogie should be completed to show that here was proof that the rebuild was feasible and had indeed started. A launch date for the project was still in the future, but something had to be ready for such an event, and it was proposed that the frame was to be used for display.

By November 1996 there was still no sign of a cylinder pattern, various sources having been approached, Swindon and the Vale of Rhiedol among them. Various financial sources had been approached unsuccessfully for funding so the search for all resources continued, including a lottery approach in a later year, but to no avail.

To further progress, it was proposed and agreed that a Steam Rail motor Group should be established under the auspices of the Great Western Society. The 'drawing office' problem was still much to the fore, additionally complicated by the fact that any young volunteer draftsmen would be metric system and CAD orientated, whereas all existing data and drawings would be Imperial. Research and data from Dr Ralph Tutton was introduced to the meeting of November 1996, when it was also confirmed that all known drawings were now to hand, and a proposed launch date of 1998 was proposed.

During 1997, the author was supplied with drawings for the wheels and horn guides, and had begun pattern-making. The axle-box drawings were also being prepared and by the 11 December meeting in 1997 the horn guide and wheel patterns were complete.

The official launch took place on 25 April 1998 so the project was now firmly established. The success of the launch was to be dampened by the sudden death of Dr Ralph Tutton the following month, his interest and enthusiasm the major factor in developments to date.

By the December 1998 committee meeting, the axle-box patterns were complete, along with the motion plate and various brackets and the author was awaiting drawings for the cylinder items. It was agreed that the car body would be repaired in the carriage shed at Didcot, stripping to be done in sections to maintain visitor interest during rebuilding. By this time construction of the frame for the power bogie was well established at Tyseley Workshops, with the horn guides cast and machined and awaiting fitting to the very substantial frame plates.

By 10 May 2000 it was reported that the car body was in much better condition than first thought, with repairs being straightforward although, as always, time consuming.

It was intended that the car body would closely follow the design of the original, using replacement timber for the bodywork, all timber treated with fire-resistant compounds and the boiler/driving compartment lined with steel sheeting. The luggage compartment adjoining the boiler compartment was similarly treated to form an effective fire barrier between the passenger compartment and the boiler area.

A trip to view the progress on the frame assembly at Tyseley was also planned, and a successful visit made. By the beginning of 2001 the cylinder-block pattern, along with the steam chest and cylinder front and back covers and gland patterns had all been completed, after further detailed attention to conform to new moulding sand requirements, and were used successfully by Cerdic Foundry, Chard, Somerset during October 2001. The castings were machined at Tyseley.

The proposed erection of the right-hand cylinder and motion assembly could now proceed, as an anomaly had come to light with the valve-gear drawings and design, and a mock-up made to ensure that the valve-gear components (outside Walschaert gear) would be made correctly the first time, and would give the correct valve events.

In the meantime, progress was being made with construction of the boiler; Israel Newton of Bradford working on the vertical cylindrical design, while various boiler fittings were being sourced at Didcot. Events were advancing with the power unit, and a stage in the rebuild is shown with the photographs following, a rolling chassis with one cylinder in place.

An early thought of restoring the coach body at Didcot had now been rejected, and so the vehicle was wrapped up and transported to the Llangollen Railway Workshops for the necessary reinstatement of the woodwork. This having been completed, the SRM group now had a complete but empty rail motor shell. A further project was now the fitting-out of the inside.

A major requirement in the list of fittings was for the seats. These were a special design with reversible backrests, so those passengers who wished to 'face the engine' could do so. By a very strange coincidence a distant member of the Society, from Australia, forwarded information that some obsolete tramcars in Adelaide were in the process of being scrapped and the seating was of the same design and by the same makers, Peters of Slough, as that required for the steam rail motor. Correspondence flowed, a container was dispatched, and the rail motor was well on course for authentic completion, once the seats had been reupholstered as the originals.

Decorated internally in the original style, even to the extent of monogrammed blinds on the windows carrying the GWR logo, all assisted by a very welcome £768,500 grant from the Lottery Fund, this authentic Edwardian relic is now up and running in service under its own power. So, on 28 May 2011 No. 93 became officially launched as a unique addition to the Great Western Society's historic locomotive fleet, a survivor from the original ninety-nine and an important link in the chain of locomotive development and design.

With the construction of a period 'running shed' to house the rail motor and its trailer car (No. 92), the project is neatly completed.

Car No. 93 against the Buffers at Reading c.1959. The mobile office with the team of the Work Study Section (CM&EEs Dept) L to R: Don Flook (CM&EEs), Jack Dowsett (Road Motor Engineers Dept), the Author (CM&EEs), Horace Rodda (CM&EEs), Fred Kitchen (Road Motor Engineers Dept), Dennis Norris (CM&EEs). Mr Robinson returned to Swindon. (Author's Collection)

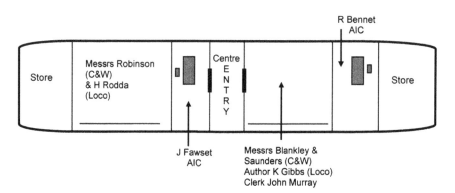

Office layout,1956, and the occupants.

The illustration from the front cover of the Great Western Society report and accounts for 2008 photographed at Didcot Rail Centre. The engine unit assembly well advanced.

Progress with assembly of the power bogie. (GWS)

Cylinder patterns for car No. 93: (a) half top and bolting face of the cylinder block; (b) various core boxes; (c) core boxes for exhaust and live steam; (d) rear cylinder cover pattern; (e) front cylinder cover pattern; (f) steam chest pattern. (Photos K. Gibbs)

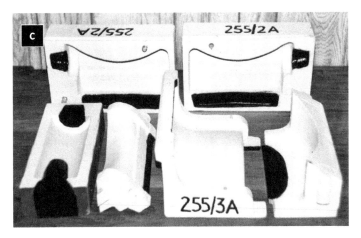

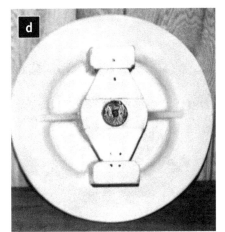

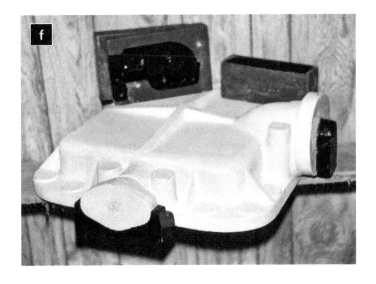

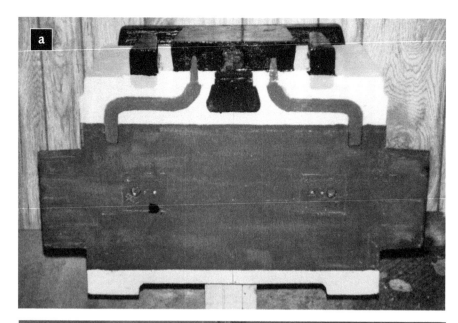

Various patterns for No. 93: (a) half cylinder pattern. Joint face showing the position of the bore and the live steam and exhaust core positions; (b) the 8in crank driving wheel pattern (4ft dia.); (c) pattern for 'Richardson' balanced slide valve; (d) axle box pattern and core boxes with the oil keep pattern and core boxes (oil keep for 'Armstrong' type oilers).

No. 93 – the opening phase of the rebuild. Stripping off the metal sheeting and the thin wooden liners underneath. The liners did much to protect the original framework from corrosion of the plating (which was not galvanised or protected in any way) and natural rot. This had maintained the wood frame in very good condition considering its age.

The cylindrical, vertical boiler shown here sprouting some of its fittings during completion.

The wood mock-up of the valve gear (Walschaerts) to establish the pivot pin and shaft length positions for correct valve events.

The crossheads await assembly.

A look into the rather restricted cab, showing the boiler and its fittings, the same as seen on a conventional locomotive firebox 'backhead', although the regulator is not usually as low as this one. Note also the coal baskets! (Photo Dennis Feltham)

Fitting the left-hand cylinder.

Power unit frame right-hand cylinder in position. Note the boiler in position (top left).

The water filler lid, the inside water tank just visible.

Pattern for the water filler lid (patterns by the author): full size templates from the enlarged drawing, cut out and stuck onto cardboard. The half template turned over for the full shape of the lid. To be cast in SG iron.

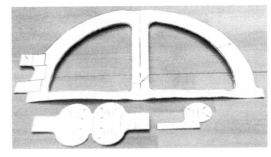

The 'roughed-out' lid under construction – all hinge items are made from layered thicknesses of ply cut out with a hole cutter and glued together.

The other half of the hinge construction – made as a 'stick', both together will simplify moulding. To be cast in SG iron.

The completed lid and hinge pattern.

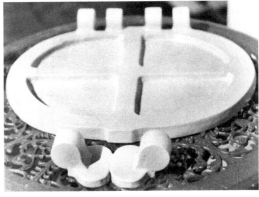

Steam rail motor passenger compartment – gas light fitting. The pattern has been made as an original gas light fitting converted for electricity: (a) original fitting and its roof ventilator. Note the fretted steel ceiling attachment and the external roof vent; (b) the inside of the fitting and glass globe; (c) patterns – the fitting showing the solid area for an electric light fitting in the centre; (d) the inside shape of the fitting.

Epilogue

While this book was being written, it was announced by the *Rail News* for September 2013 (the voice of Network Rail) that Network Rail, Bombardier, Greater Anglia, RSSB and the Department of Transport that work has begun, additionally to the proposed electrification of certain lines, for the development of powered vehicles using two different forms of batteries: lithium (iron magnesium) phosphate and hot sodium nickel salt. Extensive trials are underway. A Class 379 unit is to be the 'guinea pig'.

This is not 'new' as such, as battery-powered trains have been used for a number of years for underground railway maintenance when the main power has been switched off, but this is an attempt for main-line working. Such a train, battery powered, could work on non-electrified lines on the main system or under the wires on electrified track.

Could we see a future including a battery-powered rail motor? Who knows – the potential is wide open!

REFERENCES AND FURTHER READING

Primary Sources

Contemporary records. Great Western etc.
Details in the text of this book:
Minutes of Regular Shareholders' Meetings
Half-Yearly Reports to Proprietors
Minutes of Monthly Superintendents Meetings
Minutes of Traffic Committee Meetings
Minutes of GWR Board Meetings
Minutes of Locomotive, Carriage & Wagon Committee Meetings
1903–1935 Inclusive GWR Locomotive Allocation Registers
General Managers Reports
Minutes of The International Railway Congress Association. Eighth Session. Berne, July 1910
The Wilkinson Report 1925–6. Branch Lines and The Rail motor Car.
Locos of The GWR Part II. Rail motor Vehicles. Railway Travel & Correspondence Society, 1951
The Construction of Steam Rail motors. Transactions 1906/7. H. Nash. Swindon Engineering Society. A Swindon Works Group. G.W. Mechanics Institute.
Relevant Engineering Drawings from The Archives of 'Steam' GWR Museum, Swindon.

The Steam Rail Motor Project

Minutes of group meetings & related research papers
The author's practical involvement with the rebuild
The research of Dr Ralph Tutton

Secondary Sources

Technical Journals of the Period:

The Engineer *The Railway Gazette*

The Locomotive *The Railway Engineer*

The Great Western Railway Magazine *The Railway Magazine*

The Railway News

Further Reading references to Steam Motors:

A number of railway books have references to steam rail motors, usually one or two pages only, sometimes only a photograph. Some of those available:

H. Holcroft, *Outline of GW Loco Practice 1837–1947*, Ian Allan, 1971

J. Low, *British Steam Loco Builders*, Goose & Sons, 1975

D.J. Croft, *Nidd Valley Light Railway*, Oakwood Press

O. S. Nock, *G. W. Railway in the 20th Century*, Ian Allan, 1964

R. W. Rush, *British Steam Railcars*, Oakwood Press

F. Booker, *Great Western Railway*, David & Charles, 1977

R. Abbott, *Vertical Boiler Locos & Rail motors Built in the UK*, Oakwood Press, 1989

R. Kidner, *The Railcar 1847–1939*, Oakwood Press, 1939

ABOUT THE AUTHOR

Ken Gibbs was a fourth generation into the GWR, from his great grandfather (1849), grandfather (1875), father (1909) and himself (1944).

Apprenticed to Fitting, Turning and Steam Locomotive Erecting, he followed his grandfather in the trade, and his father as a boiler maker, from apprenticeship, into and out of the RAF, back onto the shop floor in 1953. In 1955 he moved into a staff post and was seconded to a firm of industrial consultants working in Swindon Works and later the GWR system on production studies on plant maintenance. This entailed working and supervising two teams in a number of the Steam Maintenance area Workshops and Sub Depots (many inherited from absorbed railway companies). He then became Area Assistant for the Southwest on departure from the consultants, which involved re-layout and selection of plant for the non-ferrous foundry at Swindon Works.

He retired early, joining the Great Western Society at Didcot and the *Firefly* Project and Trust, where he became involved with the broad-gauge replica's twenty-three-year construction-from-scratch project, making, with the exception of the wheels and splasher beading, every pattern for every casting used, from the small maker's plate to the cylinders. He was also involved with patterns, fitting and machining for components for the *King, Hall/Saint* conversion and the Steam Rail motor, and with patterns and components for several other railway groups, as well as those for Didcot Great Western Society.

By the Author

Steam Workshops of the Great Western Railway, The History Press, 2014
The Great Western Railway: How it Grew, Amberley Publishing, 2012
The Steam Locomotive: An Engineering History, Amberley Publishing, 2012
Swindon Works: Apprentice in Steam, Oxford Railway Publishing, 1988 (reprinted by Amberley Publishing, 2013)

Plus magazine articles dealing with: military history, military model engineering, machine tool hobby engineering, railway history and heritage railway wood and metalwork (i.e. pattern-making for carriage and locomotive components and associated machining and fitting operations) over a period of about fifty years.

Other titles published by The History Press

The Steam Workshops of the Great Western Railway

KEN GIBBS

The nineteenth century was a time of innovation and expansion. At the head of the race up was the iconic Great Western Railway. Retired railwayman Ken Gibbs presents a portrait of GWR works from Brunel to the final days of steam in the mid-twentieth century and beyond.

978 0 7509 5912 4

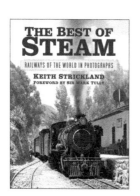

The Best of Steam
Railways of the World in Photographs

KEITH STRICKLAND

After forty years of adventuring around the world's remaining steam railways, Keith Strickland has compiled the very best of his vast collection of railway photographs. From Austria to Zimbabwe and beyond, this book reflects the unique atmosphere of steam trains, and records an era which is now history

978 0 7524 9939 0

The Great Western Railway in the First World War

SANDRA GITTINS

In August 1914 the GWR was plunged into war, the like of which this country had never experienced before. Over the years that followed life changed beyond measure, both for the men sent away to fight and the women who took on new roles at home. Sandra Gittins traces the GWR's wartime story from the early, optimistic days through the subsequent difficult years of the Great War.

978 0 7524 5632 4

Visit our website and discover thousands of other History Press books.
www.thehistorypress.co.uk